"Until you go to Kentucky
and with your own eyes behold a Derby,
you ain't never been nowheres
and you ain't seen nothin'."

—Irvin S. Cobb

The Kentucky

101 Reasons to Love™
America's Favorite Horse Race

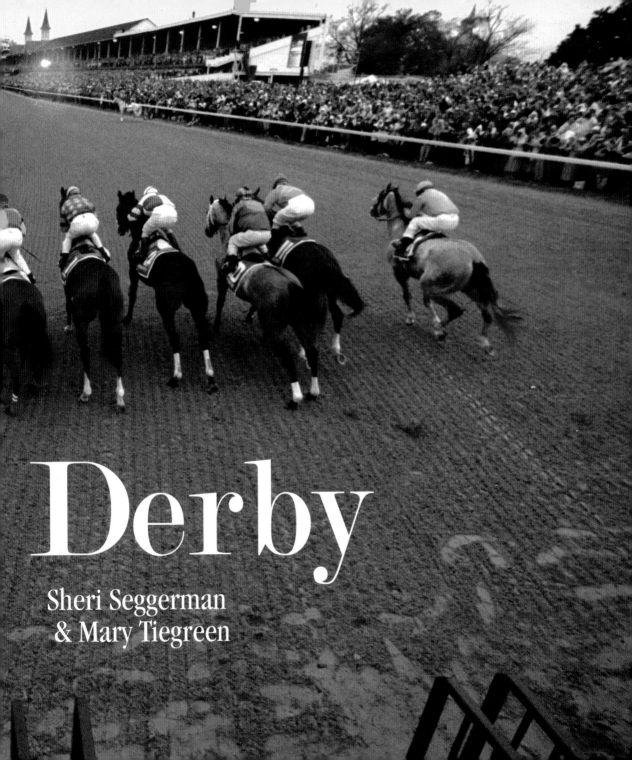

Derby

Sheri Seggerman
& Mary Tiegreen

Introduction

The Kentucky Derby is not *just* "the most exciting two minutes in sports." It is so much larger than that. It is an entire culture, from the Derby Ball to the barns on the backstretch, from the breeding shed to the starting gate. It is cocktails at the Brown and breakfast at Wagner's. It's the historical displays at the Derby Museum and the wilted roses left at the base of the Barbaro statue. It is elegant and raucous, genteel and democratic. It is soaked in tradition, yet it spins a new story each year.

Like many horse enthusiasts, I first acquired the moniker of "horse crazy" in childhood. I grew up in a small Midwestern town with a racetrack at the fairgrounds and galloped my pony in a one-horse race across the finish line of the Kentucky Derby time after time to the roaring cheers of an empty grandstand. When my grandmother gave me a magazine subscription to the *Blood-Horse* for my birthday, I followed the contenders to the first Saturday in May and was thrilled to see the black-and-white image of my favorite, Carry Back, sail across the finish line on our TV screen.

My father indulged my newfound interest. He used to take me to Arlington Park, where he sat in the clubhouse with his martini while I ran the steps to watch the horses being saddled in the paddock and parade down the track. Breathlessly I'd barrel in to tell him who would win the race. He'd look at me quizzically and place a $2 bet on my choice. I remember the first horse I ever bet on was Black Destroyer. In the middle of the race, he broke his bridle and was led off the track. I was thrilled! He was the Black Stallion and no one could rein in this horse! My father once took me to stay with family friends who lived in Los Angeles and owned racehorses. I spent a week going to morning workouts at Santa Anita. Heaven for a 12-year-old girl. Years later, with my father, I won the double quinella. He was proud of me, and I was hooked.

Now grown up and still horse crazy, I try to read every horse-racing book released. I have attended the Hall of Fame inductions, watched races at Saratoga, and traveled to several runnings of the Breeders' Cup. I've attended the Fasig-Tipton yearling sales, visited many famous horse farms, bet on the Arlington Million, and joined the Louisville Thoroughbred Club. I've hosted several Derby parties in my home, acquired a taste for mint juleps, and introduced many friends to my world of horse racing.

But until 2009, I had never been to the Derby. It was a childhood dream I had to fulfill. I needed to be there. I needed to know what John Steinbeck really meant when he said, "The Kentucky Derby, whatever it is—a race, an emotion, a turbulence, an explosion—is one of the most beautiful and violent and satisfying things I have ever experienced."

And after attending I think I *did* understand.

I did not bet on Mine That Bird and, like many, can't understand why. I love a long shot, and there were clues to this thrilling upset—the most obvious being that his sire was Birdstone, who kept the Triple Crown from Smarty Jones in 2004.

I walked away with empty pockets, but it didn't matter. Seeing Calvin Borel stand in his stirrups after the wire, crop held high in salute to the moment, all I could feel was a euphoria for the horse, the jockey, the trainer and owner, the women at Kroger who stitched the rose blanket, the mass of humanity who stood and sang "My Old Kentucky Home," the balloon handlers in the Pegasus Parade, the waitress at Wagner's who called me "honey," and the child who stroked the nose of the statue of Big Brown. I have never felt so much a part of a spectator sport. For this I have to thank the entire city of Louisville. I have never seen so much community effort surrounding an event. I have never felt this much warmth and comradeship with strangers. Perhaps it rests in childhood fantasy, but how often does something live up to your world of make-believe?

—*Sheri Seggerman*

The Dream

Every horse that enters the starting gate in the
Kentucky Derby is carrying the prescribed weight
and many people's dreams: the breeder who hoped
for a Derby Day horse, the vet who attended the
birth, the stable hands who kept the filly or colt in
clean bedding with its dam, the owner who saw
"the look of eagles" at the yearling sale, the exercise
rider who rated her in the early mist, the hot walker
who patiently cooled him down, the groom who
brought his coat to a gleam before the race, the
trainer who placed the saddle on her back, the
jockey who was boosted up in the paddock, and the
millions of spectators around the world. That's a
lot to carry a mile and a quarter, but that's what's
necessary to win.

2 The Vision

The Kentucky Derby was the dream of Meriwether Lewis Clark Jr. after a trip to Europe exploring possible ways to revive the horse-racing industry in Kentucky. Enamored of Britain's Epsom Derby, a premier race open to top three-year-old colts and fillies, he hoped to create such a race in Kentucky. With 320 backers and a lease on 80 acres of land owned by his uncles, the Churchills, the Kentucky Derby was born.

The first running was on May 17, 1875, before an enthusiastic crowd of 10,000 spectators. Many sat in the newly built grandstand for the hefty fee of $1. Members sat in the glass-enclosed Jockey Club sipping mint juleps, while others shelled out 50 cents to ride into the infield. A special section was provided for ladies who wished to be distanced from gambling.

H. P. McGrath had entered two colts in the Derby: one was his favored horse, Chesapeake; the other, Aristides, who was to set the pace and tire the early speed. As Aristides' jockey, Oliver Lewis, began to slow down around the final turn, Chesapeake was nowhere in sight. With a yell from McGrath, Lewis loosened the reins and Aristides galloped to victory. Chesapeake finished eighth.

In 1883, the name "Churchill Downs" was coined in a newspaper article. The name was officially incorporated in 1942.

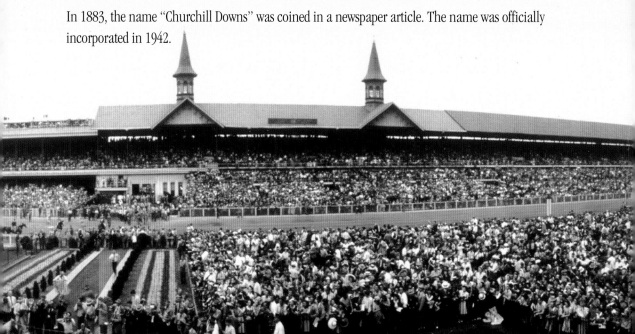

3 Mr. Kentucky Derby

Generally considered the person most responsible for making the Kentucky Derby the premier horse-racing event of the nation, Colonel Matt Winn knew how to cajole the rich and famous, entice the top horsemen, and build excitement for the racing fan. Winn became vice president of Churchill Downs in 1902 and then president. Having watched the first Derby at age 13 sitting in his father's grocery truck in the infield, he attended the first 75 Derbies, until his death in 1949. It is no wonder he was honored with the nickname "Mr. Kentucky Derby."

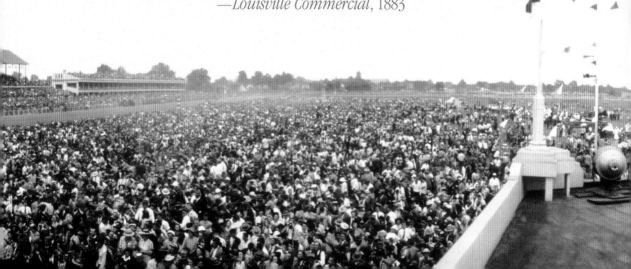

"The crowd in the grandstand sent out
a volume of voice, and the crowd in the field
took it up and carried it from
boundary to boundary of
Churchill Downs."

—*Louisville Commercial*, 1883

4 Bluegrass Country

Central Kentucky is as famous for its bluegrass as it is for its horses. In fact, it is the limestone lying under the rolling hills that provides the rich soil shown to enhance the skeletal development and metabolism of horses that graze there. Whether this is the secret or not, more than 100 of the winners of the Kentucky Derby were Kentucky bred.

Before or after the Kentucky Derby, treat yourself to a drive through the bluegrass country. Take the marked scenic routes through Midway, Versailles, and Paris, Kentucky. Follow the miles of groomed green hills lined with black and white board fences, limestone walls, and tree-canopied lanes leading to historic horse farms. Watch for the plaques on the iron gates with names like Claiborne, Spendthrift, and Calumet. Stop and watch a new crop of foals play out a make-believe Derby before dashing back to their dams for reassurance. Only then will you understand the well-tended dreams of a Derby hopeful.

5 Living the Lyrics

In Dan Fogelberg's popular song "The Run for the Roses," a foal's life is chronicled as he prepares for the Kentucky Derby. The line "It's the chance of a lifetime in a lifetime of chance" is a philosophy we all should live by, for as he goes on to say, "It's high time you joined in the dance." It may be the best reason ever voiced to attend the Kentucky Derby.

6 The Derby Train

For years, the preferred form of transportation to the Kentucky Derby was by train, and for many it still is. Train enthusiasts spend months decorating and preparing ornate Derby cars, and fans ride the rails to Louisville holding their Derby galas aboard the train before settling into the Pullman cars for the night. Railway aficionados line the tracks from the hills of Virginia to downtown Midway, Kentucky, to capture movies and photos of these beautiful cars.

Each year, a crew paints and details a special railroad car to carry the governor of Kentucky, and a group of celebrities and friends from Frankfort to Louisville. For the rest of us, there's NetJets, or if you're a friend of Funny Cide, a yellow school bus.

7 The Grand Hotels of Louisville

If your Derby dreams include experiencing old Louisville elegance, check into the Brown or Seelbach Hotel in downtown Louisville. These historic hotels catered to the likes of Elizabeth Taylor, the Duke of Windsor, and Joan Crawford; soprano Lily Pons once checked into the Brown with her pet lion. Originally opened in 1923, the Brown has recently gone through a major renovation but retains its original English Renaissance style.

The Seelbach was the setting for the wedding in F. Scott Fitzgerald's *The Great Gatsby,* and Fitzgerald was a frequent guest, lured by the opulence and parties. He liked to sit in the Rookwood Pottery Bavarian Rathskeller, sipping bourbon and smoking cigars. The Oakroom, the Seelbach's dark oak four-star dining room, was originally the men's billiard parlor and catered to Al Capone and his friends.

The enthusiasm of both the staff and guests makes for nonstop Derby chatter in the bars and restaurants. If you're not staying in a grand hotel, stop in for a drink or dinner, catch a preview of Derby fashion, and wear that fleeting aura of luxury on Derby Day.

8 Running for the Roses

Surrounded by press photographers and the roar of the crowd, a steaming thoroughbred is led into the winner's circle as a garland of roses is thrown across its withers. The first roses were given out to the winner of the Derby in 1896, but the roses were pink and white. In 1904, the red rose became the official flower of the Derby, and in 1925 sports columnist Bill Corum coined the phrase "Run for the Roses." The blanket of roses was introduced in 1932, garnishing winner Burgoo King.

For years, Kingsley Walker Florist constructed the garland, but since 1987, a local Kroger grocery store has stitched the 554 roses into the green satin background and put it on display for the public on Derby Eve.

There is a certain reverence for the blanket's construction as the women at Kroger, wearing their horseshoe diamond bracelets, hand-stitch each rose before a crowd of spectators paying homage. The garland has the seal of the commonwealth on one side and the twin spires with the number of years the Derby has been run stitched on the other.

There is a crown of roses on the garland, with a rose for each horse running and a single rose that rises to the sky in the center, signifying the heart required to win the Derby. The jockey receives a bouquet of 60 roses during the winner's circle ceremonies.

At left, jockey Mike Smith smiles atop Giacomo as he's presented with the garland of roses after winning the Kentucky Derby on May 7, 2005.

At right, assembling the garland for the 2009 Derby

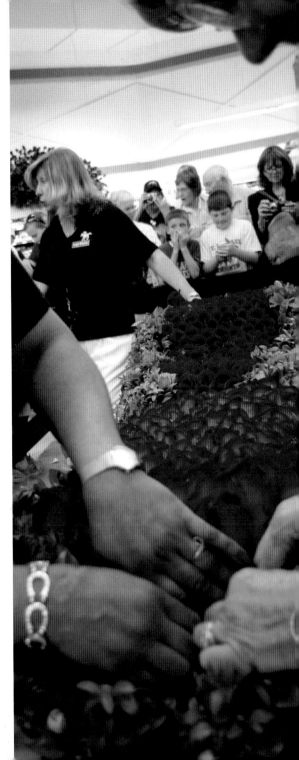

9 Old Bones

Everyone loves an underdog, and Exterminator is the Cinderella of the Kentucky Derby. Willis Kilmer had his trainer purchase a horse two weeks before the 1918 Kentucky Derby to be used as a workout companion and pacemaker for his beloved Sun Briar. When the trainer came back with Exterminator, a large, gangly brown gelding, Kilmer was not impressed. The horse was so large and bony that over the years he earned the nicknames of "Old Bones" and "the Galloping Hat Rack." Yet the gelding did his job and pushed Sun Briar in workouts. As Derby Day approached, Sun Briar was unfit to race. Colonel Matt Winn convinced Kilmer to run Exterminator in Sun Briar's place.

Although Exterminator had raced four times as a two-year-old and won twice, when jockey Willie Knapp guided him toward the Kentucky Derby starting line, Exterminator had yet to race as a three-year-old. On a muddy track, before an astonished crowd, Old Bones moved from fifth to second, and he went on to win by a length!

Over the next six years, Old Bones showed the world that looks weren't everything as he won races from six furlongs to 2¼ miles, on fast tracks, muddy tracks, and everything in between. He was a quiet, determined horse and was said to stare down horses that were making a commotion at the starting wire, sidling up to them to make them stand still. He had several jockeys and trainers, but Kilmer said Exterminator always made up for their failures, focusing on the finish line at all times.

Over his racing years, Exterminator became a national hero, winning 50 of his 100 races. Retired at nine, Exterminator became attached to a Shetland pony named Peanuts and lived out his life frolicking in pastures with his friend. At 28, Old Bones made his final appearance with Peanuts at Belmont Park to help raise $25 million in war bonds. At age 29, Exterminator hosted a birthday party for the children of his village, eating a sugar cake with carrot candles and allowing some of the youngest children to sit on his back. The classic children's book *Old Bones the Wonder Horse*, written by Mildred Mastin Pace, was published in 1955.

Exterminator and Sun Briar (on the rail)
working out at Saratoga in 1919

"If I chose one horse and called him the greatest—that would start a controversy. But what sort of Irishman would I be if I didn't start a controversy, now and then? I choose Exterminator, because when greatness is reckoned, the factors entering into it are speed, courage, stamina, intelligence, and perhaps, more importantly, durability."

—Matt Winn, Mr. Kentucky Derby, 1945

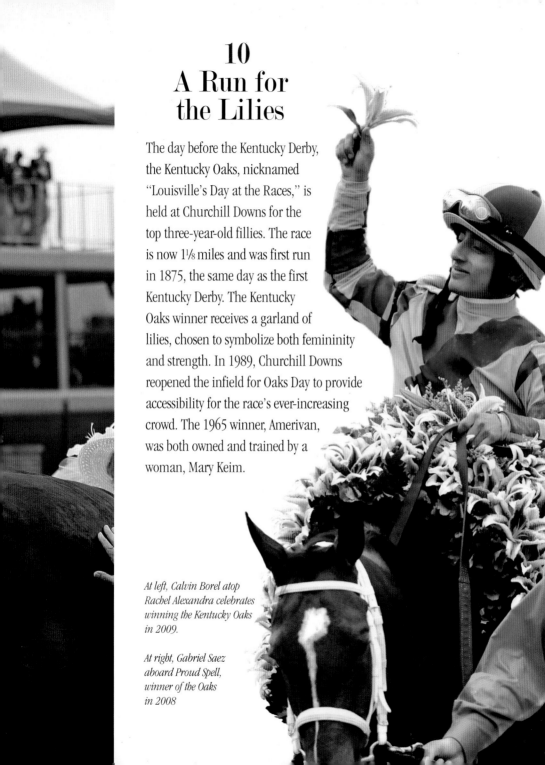

10
A Run for the Lilies

The day before the Kentucky Derby, the Kentucky Oaks, nicknamed "Louisville's Day at the Races," is held at Churchill Downs for the top three-year-old fillies. The race is now 1⅛ miles and was first run in 1875, the same day as the first Kentucky Derby. The Kentucky Oaks winner receives a garland of lilies, chosen to symbolize both femininity and strength. In 1989, Churchill Downs reopened the infield for Oaks Day to provide accessibility for the race's ever-increasing crowd. The 1965 winner, Amerivan, was both owned and trained by a woman, Mary Keim.

At left, Calvin Borel atop Rachel Alexandra celebrates winning the Kentucky Oaks in 2009.

At right, Gabriel Saez aboard Proud Spell, winner of the Oaks in 2008

11 The Holy Grail

At the finish of each Kentucky Derby, horse-racing fans leave the track hoping this will be the year for a Triple Crown winner. Perhaps the most athletic achievement for any horse, the Triple Crown is made up of three races: the Kentucky Derby, referred to as the first jewel in the crown; the Preakness, run two weeks later at Pimlico Racetrack in Baltimore, Maryland; and the Belmont Stakes, held three weeks after the Preakness at Belmont Park in Elmont, New York. To win the roses at the Kentucky Derby, the contenders race 1 1/4 miles; for the black-eyed Susans at the Preakness, they run 1 3/16 miles; and to claim the blanket of white carnations at the Belmont Stakes, they go 1 1/2 miles.

A horse with the stamina and versatility required to win all of these races is a rarity. Only 11 horses have won the Triple Crown, and no horse has achieved the feat since 1978.

For the horse-racing fan, stamina and versatility are required when it comes to the official cocktails of each competition: mint juleps at the Derby, black-eyed susans at the Preakness, and the belmont breeze at the Belmont.

Jockey Ron Turcotte, aboard Secretariat, takes a look at the field many lengths behind as they make the final turn before winning the Belmont Stakes and the 1973 Triple Crown.

12
The Kentucky Derby Museum

Adjacent to the grounds of Churchill Downs, the Kentucky Derby Museum is filled with historic photos and colorful exhibits. If you think you have the stamina, you can hoist yourself up in the stirrups of a metal horse and, with your race projected on a screen in front, attempt to stay in full jockey stance for the entire two minutes to win the race. Sound easy? Try it. While your legs are still wobbling, go into the time capsule, where you can choose whichever Derby intrigues you and watch the official film footage. Upstairs there is a starting gate, where you can climb up onto the incredibly small racing saddle and get your picture taken as you break from the gate. Afterward, be sure to go into the main oval in the center of the museum, where on the half hour visitors are treated to 360 degrees of Kentucky Derby excitement. The multimedia extravaganza includes interviews; shots of the backstretch, the crowd, and the infield; as well as a video of the most recent race played out around you. This is such a beautiful spectacle that patrons are often wiping tears from their eyes as they leave. The museum is open every day except Thanksgiving, Christmas Eve, Christmas, Oaks Day, and Derby Day.

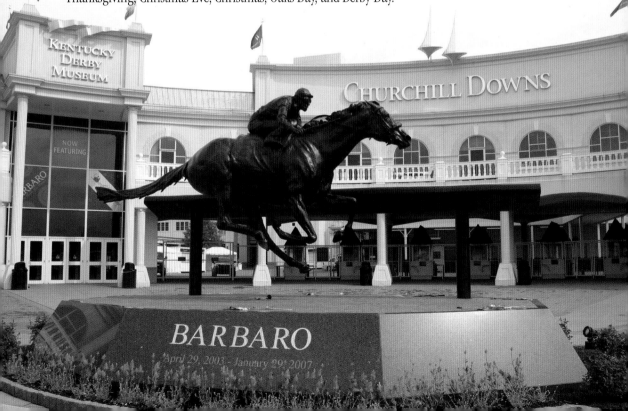

13
The Kentucky Horse Park

Only 60 minutes from Churchill Downs is the Kentucky Horse Park, 1,224 groomed acres dedicated to the love of all things equine and the home of the 2010 World Equestrian Games. At the gate

are the grave and memorial to Man o'War, and as you pass through the International Museum of the Horse, you can view the trophy collection

of racing dynasty Calumet Farm. Funny Cide, the 2003 Kentucky Derby winner, is stabled in the Hall of Champions waiting for racing fans to pay their respects. The famous racehorses Da Hoss and Cigar also reside at the park. There are trail rides, horse-drawn wagons, frequent horse shows, and a daily Parade of Breeds. If you're looking to adopt a retired racehorse, the Kentucky wing of the Thoroughbred Retirement Foundation is also on the grounds.

14
Track Conditions

Different horses prefer different running surfaces and track conditions. As several upper-echelon tracks have recently switched to synthetic surfaces, performance at Churchill Downs with its dirt surface now poses a new question for the handicapper and trainer. Prior to synthetics, the main question was one of condition. The Kentucky Derby has been run on a sloppy track five times, and a muddy track seven. Dirt was the predominant racing surface in the United States, but now most preps in the West are run on synthetic. This adds one more element to decipher in the art of Derby horse wagering.

15
Going the Distance

From the starting gate to the finish wire, with your eyes on the oval and your heart in your throat, you cheer as your chosen favorite maneuvers through traffic to be first under the wire.

The original length of the Kentucky Derby was 1½ miles until 1896, when it was shortened to 1¼ miles. The shorter length attracted more competitors from other states and helped ensure that the Derby would become the preeminent horse race in the country for three-year-olds.

"Horse sense is the
thing a horse has
which keeps it from
betting on people."

—W. C. Fields

16 Handicapping

With a *Daily Racing Form* in hand, prep races reviewed on YouTube, and a few tips from insiders, the true handicapper will plot the Kentucky Derby furlong by furlong. Taking into account the horses with early speed, the morning workouts, the distances at which each horse preps, the Beyer Speed Figures, its dosage, the lapse since its last race, the horse's pedigree, its post position, the jockey, the trainer, whether they prep on synthetic or dirt, and the competition, the handicapper places a calculated wager. Hopefully the professionals will do better than the fan who chooses three horses for a trifecta based on the initials of her ex-husbands.

17 Future Wagering

In 1999, the Kentucky Derby made pari-mutuel history when it offered future wagering months prior to the event. Three four-day betting periods are available, one each in February, March, and April. A $2 minimum bet can be placed on 23 Derby contenders and a mutuel field at usually much higher odds than will be available on Derby Day.

18 The Pick Six

If you want to leave the Derby feeling as if you won the race, it's easy! Just get to the betting window five races prior to the Derby, buy a pick-six ticket, and correctly choose the winner of each race plus the Kentucky Derby. If you're right, next year you may be able to afford to sit in Millionaires Row.

19 The Full Card

On Derby Day, there are many races on the card including graded stakes. The Kentucky Derby is run toward the end of the day, giving you plenty of time to witness high-class thoroughbreds running in high-stakes races prior to choosing the winner of the Derby.

20 Considering the Odds-on Favorite

The odds-on favorite is a horse that runs at less than even money, such as 4–5, and pays a very minimal amount. In the Kentucky Derby, there have been only 32 odds-on favorites, of which only 17 have won, and 11 have come in second.

21
Morning Workouts
on the Backstretch

If you can figure out a way to visit the backstretch of
Churchill Downs for morning workouts during Derby
week, any begging you had to do will be worth it. With
trainers and clockers leaning on the rail, workout riders
hurrying to grab their next mounts, grooms hosing off
steaming horses, the sound of hoofbeats, and galloping
horses emerging from the morning fog, this is heaven for
the true aficionado. The Derby contenders will be wearing
special saddle blankets, if you can't pick them out by the
clicks of the camera shutters.

22
World-Renowned Trainers

At the Kentucky Derby, you will be surrounded by some of the most famous trainers in the world, each with one to as many as five hopefuls going to the gate for different owners. Some you will see on the rail or on horseback during morning workouts, and on Derby Day they will lead their horses over from the barn. They will be saddling their horses in the paddock and sitting in boxes in the grandstand with the owners, and one will be crossing the track to the winner's circle.

Ben A. Jones is the winningest trainer with six Derby victories, followed by H. J. "Dick" Thompson and D. Wayne Lucas with four each. Sunny Fitzsimmons, Max Hirsch, and Bob Baffert each have three Kentucky Derby wins.

23
The Feminine Mystique

Although the Kentucky Oaks is restricted to top fillies, the Kentucky Derby is open to colts, geldings, and fillies. Only 39 fillies have run in the Derby, but 10 have finished in the money. So don't discount the ladies, as three of these fillies came in first, beginning with Regret in 1915. Genuine Risk, the 1980 winner, was the first filly to win that was owned by a woman, Diana Firestone. The filly Winning Colors won the 1988 Derby.

24
Long Shots

There is nothing more exhilarating than seeing your long shot make his move while the commentators continue to babble on about the favorites.

Donerail: 91–1
wins 1913 Kentucky Derby, pays $184.90 to win

Mine That Bird: 51–1
wins 2009 Kentucky Derby, pays $103.20 to win

Giacomo: 50–1
wins 2005 Kentucky Derby, pays $102.60 to win

Gallahadion: 35–1
wins 1940 Kentucky Derby, pays $72.40 to win

Charismatic: 31–1
wins 1999 Kentucky Derby, pays $64.60 to win

Proud Clarion: 30–1
wins 1967 Kentucky Derby, pays $62.20 to win

Exterminator: 30–1
wins 1918 Kentucky Derby, pays $61.20 to win

Dark Star: 25–1
wins 1953 Kentucky Derby, pays $51.80 to win

Thunder Gulch: 25–1
wins 1995 Kentucky Derby, pays $51 to win

Long shot Thunder Gulch, far right, ridden by Gary Stevens, wins the 121st Kentucky Derby, May 6, 1995.

25 Sir Barton

A grandson of the 1893 English Triple Crown winner, Isinglass, Sir Barton went to the post six times as a two-year-old but never won a race. In 1918, he was sold to Canadian businessman J. K. Ross. Ross purchased him to be a running mate for his Derby hopeful, Billy Kelly. Still a maiden and unraced as a three-year-old, he was entered in the 1919 Kentucky Derby with Billy Kelly to break fast and wear out the field. Instead, Sir Barton broke to the front and led the race wire to wire, with Johnny Loftus in the saddle, leaving the favorites Billy Kelly and Eternal in his wake.

In 1919, there was no name for the Triple Crown and the Preakness was held only four days after the Derby. Ross entered Sir Barton in the Preakness, and once again the horse wired the field. With the horse on his game, Ross entered Sir Barton in the Withers Stakes in New York a few days later, and once again he triumphed. The Belmont Stakes was not far away, so Ross kept him in New York, where Sir Barton won the Belmont and set a record for the 1⅜ miles, the distance of the Belmont in 1919. This all happened in the space of 32 days, and Sir Barton was voted Horse of the Year; yet his name is not a household word. Shortly after Sir Barton's triumphs, the Michael Jordan of horse racing, Man o'War, came on the scene and captured the nation's imagination. Eventually a match race was set, where Sir Barton, sore-footed and tired, was soundly defeated by the new superstar.

In Man o'War's wake, Sir Barton was forgotten by the media and was retired to stand at Audley Farm. He was eventually sold and served his country as a stallion in the U.S. Remount Service. He spent his last years on a ranch in Wyoming, passed away in 1937, and was buried by his paddock. Sir Barton was inducted into the National Thoroughbred Racing Hall of Fame in 1957, and he is now heralded as the first winner of the Triple Crown. His remains have been moved to a park in Douglas, Wyoming, where a simple statue has been erected in his honor.

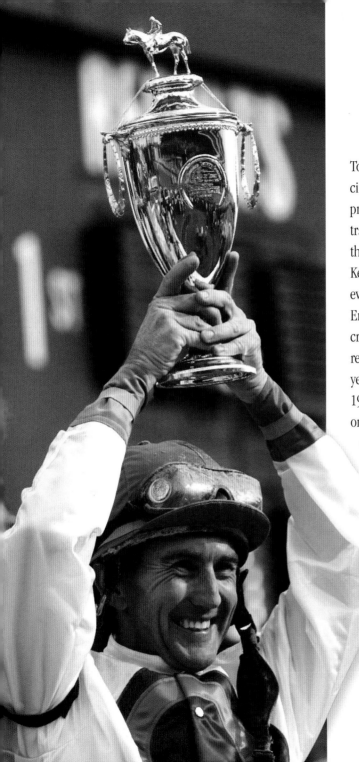

26
The Golden Trophy

To add to the decadence of the rose-laden winner's circle ceremonies, owners of the winners are presented with a hand-crafted solid gold trophy, a tradition first introduced at the 50th running of the Kentucky Derby, in 1924. It is believed that the Kentucky Derby is the only annual sporting event with a solid gold trophy. Artisans at New England Sterling work hundreds of hours to create the cup. The trophy's style has remained generally the same over the years, with one major exception. In 1999, the 14-karat gold horseshoe on the trophy was turned upward as, according to horse-racing lore, a horseshoe should always be hung points up so one's luck cannot run out.

Jerry Bailey holds the trophy high after piloting Grindstone to a photo-finish win in the 122nd Kentucky Derby, on May 4, 1996.

27
A Kaleidoscope
of Silks

The jockeys never have to worry about what to wear to the Kentucky Derby. Dressed in a splash of color and pattern, each rider is required to wear the owner's registered silks. These brilliant colors that add extra pizzazz to the event are now made of nylon rather than the traditional silk. The colors most often seen in the winner's circle were the Calumet Farm silks, devil's red with royal blue stripes on the arms. Perhaps the best-dressed winners were Secretariat and Riva Ridge, who both wore blue-and-white checkered hoods to match jockey Ron Turcotte's Meadow Farm ensemble of royal blue and white.

At left, Gary Stevens on
1995 winner, Thunder Gulch

At right, Pat Day

28
Keeping the Promise

In 1924, Rosa Hoots was so sure her colt would win the Derby, she arrived with a box of cigars for Colonel Matt Winn, the president of the track. You see, it had to do with Useeit. Rosa's husband had been banned from horse racing when he refused to part with his beloved mare in a claiming race. The next year on his deathbed, he made Rosa promise she would breed Useeit to the famous Kentucky stallion Black Toney. She fulfilled her husband's wish. The result: a jet black foal Rosa named after the oil on her land in Oklahoma—Black Gold, winner of the 50th Kentucky Derby.

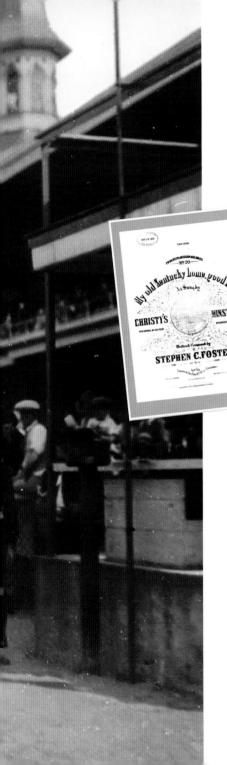

29
Kentucky's Anthem

No one is sure when "My Old Kentucky Home" was first played at the Kentucky Derby, but there are references to the crowd singing it in celebration of the Kentucky-bred Behave Yourself's victory in 1921. Now a tradition as the horses pass before the grandstand prior to the race, it is the one peaceful moment when the cheering stops and the crowd rises in unison to sing while the University of Louisville Marching Band plays. A transcendence comes over the crowd, tears are wiped away with the last refrain, and the simultaneous roar from the stands punctuates the last note.

In 1982, Churchill Downs created the Stephen Foster Handicap to honor the composer.

"I've talked to a few guys—Gary Stevens, Robby Albarado, Jerry Bailey—that's just to name a few. They've pretty much given me the same advice: Don't cry when they sing 'My Old Kentucky Home.'"

—Joe Talamo, when asked if he had received any advice from veteran jockeys before riding in his first Kentucky Derby

Black Gold is led to the winner's circle after capturing the 50th Kentucky Derby, on May 17, 1924.

30
Hat Watching

There is no greater venue for the latent haberdasher than Derby Day in Louisville. Whether designed in the studios of Chanel in Paris or by Fred in his basement apartment in Versailles, Kentucky, an eye-catching array of headdresses will greet you at the Derby. There are contests galore for the best Derby hat, and participants pull out the stops from mechanical to mammoth, from crinoline to cryptic. If you have great seats to watch the race, you may want to bring a booster seat just in case the lady in front of you has built a bountiful bonnet.

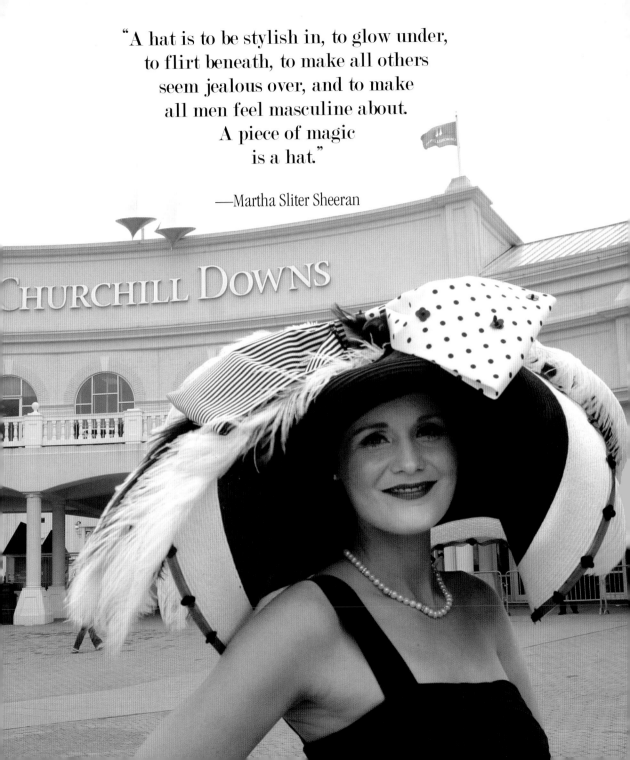

"A hat is to be stylish in, to glow under, to flirt beneath, to make all others seem jealous over, and to make all men feel masculine about. A piece of magic is a hat."

—Martha Sliter Sheeran

31 Mint Juleps

Place your bets early so you can throw caution to the wind and enjoy the tradition of the mint julep, a heady concoction of mint, simple syrup, and bourbon, on Derby Day. The julep was introduced in North America in the 1700s and was often the early morning choice of farmers to prepare for a long day of work.

The silver spoon is overrated compared to the joys of the sterling silver mint julep cup. There is really no better way to sip this drink, with the sweat of the cold silver in hand and the chilled sweetness on your lips.

In 1951, the silver mint julep cup became an official part of the Derby tradition. At the Winner's Party following the Derby, the governor of Kentucky will raise a sterling silver cup decorated with a garland and a horseshoe in honor of the winner. This cup remains at Churchill Downs, where there is one silver cup for each winner of the Kentucky Derby.

> "There is nothing better than a mint julep to bring relief from the pains and pressures of summertime."
>
> — Truman Capote

32 Derby Glasses

As you take the last sip of your mint julep at the Derby, be sure to remember to carry home the original glass. Derby glasses are very collectible and have been in production since 1938. The first "official" Derby glass, from 1939, is valued at thousands of dollars. Due to a concern about broken glass at the track, the 1940 and 1941 "glasses" were aluminum tumblers. In response to the aluminum shortage during World War II, the Beetleware Company manufactured a ceramic-type tumbler from 1942 to 1944. In 1945, there were three versions of the glass, and in 1946 and 1947, a blank glass was used. Since 1948, a glass with a new logo has appeared each year. The glass for the 129th Kentucky Derby contains a misprint in the original run. Burgoo King is marked as a Triple Crown Winner, and War Admiral is not. It's easy to date each glass in a collection, as the list of all the previous Derby winners is printed on the back.

33 Bourbon

Bourbon is the elixir of the Kentucky Derby. If you're looking for the bourbon to fill your mint julep cup, head for the Bluegrass State. More than 95 percent of all bourbon is made in Kentucky. On the Bourbon Trail you can visit eight different distilleries, including Wild Turkey, Maker's Mark, and Woodford Reserve. Be sure that your horse knows the way to carry the sleigh, as there's a tasting room at each stop.

34 Gallant Fox

The winner of the 1930 Kentucky Derby and Triple Crown, "the Fox of Belair" was an imposing and beautiful large bay colt with white socks, a white blaze, and one walleye. He was sired by Sir Gallahad at Belair Stud and foaled out of Marguerite at Claiborne Farm in 1927. Trained by Sunny Fitzsimmons and ridden by Earl Sande, who came out of retirement to do so, Gallant Fox won the Kentucky Derby—making Sande the only jockey since Isaac Murphy to win the Derby three times. Just prior to the Belmont Stakes, Sande was in a car accident, but he rode Gallant Fox to victory despite his injuries. Gallant Fox was often compared to Man o'War for his stamina and speed. His fans claimed it was the walleye that scared other horses as he pulled close and stared them down.

35
Champions of Champions

As the Derby contenders parade in front of the grandstand, you witness the culmination of the phrase "breed the best to the best and hope for the best."

Winner of the 1930 Kentucky Derby under jockey Earl Sande, Gallant Fox went on to win the yet-to-be-official Triple Crown. Retired at the end of the season, Gallant Fox stood at stud for 22 years and sired Omaha, the winner of the Triple Crown in 1935. Although Gallant Fox was the only Triple Crown winner to sire another, several other Derby winners had offspring that followed in their hoofprints as Derby winners.

Sire	Colt
Halma (1895)	Alan-a-Dale (1902)
Bubbling Over (1926)	Burgoo King (1932)
Reigh Count (1928)	Count Fleet (1943)
Bold Venture (1936)	Assault (1946)
Bold Venture (1936)	Middleground (1950)
Pensive (1944)	Ponder (1949)
Count Fleet (1943)	Count Turf (1951)
Ponder (1949)	Needles (1956)
Determine (1954)	Decidedly (1962)
Swaps (1955)	Chateaugay (1963)
Seattle Slew (1977)	Swale (1984)
Unbridled (1990)	Grindstone (1996)

At right, Swale, son of Seattle Slew, wins the 1984 Kentucky Derby.
At left, Gallant Fox, with Earl Sande up, wears the roses after winning
the 1930 Kentucky Derby.

36 Prep Races

Just like following your team to the Super Bowl or the NCAA tournament, in the months leading up to the Kentucky Derby you can watch the Derby hopefuls as they run their prep races. You can scrutinize their racing styles, their competition, and how they handle different surfaces and longer distances as they develop into Derby contenders. Twelve winners of the Florida Derby have gone on to win the Kentucky Derby, as have 11 from the Wood Memorial and the Blue Grass Stakes. Nine from the now defunct Flamingo Stakes and eight from the Santa Anita Derby have also won.

37 Choosing a Name

Whenever you're at the races, it's fun to scan the names and see if you just have a hunch—something from your childhood, your mother's maiden name, or the fulfillment of a lifelong dream. A racehorse is often named by combining an aspect of the name of its sire and the name of its dam, such as Kentucky Derby winners Funny Cide by Distorted Humor out of Belle's Good Cide, Mine That Bird by Birdstone out of Mining My Own, Whiskery by Whisk Broom II out of Prudery, Foolish Pleasure by What A Pleasure out of Fool-Me-Not, and Count Fleet by Reigh Count out of Quickly.

Smarty Jones, second from right, ridden by jockey Stewart Elliott, takes the lead in the Arkansas Derby, April 10, 2004. He remained undefeated in six races.

38 Bellying Up to a
Bowl of Burgoo

Always on the menu at Derby parties and the traditional fare of Kentucky hardboots, burgoo is a thick stew that often includes mutton, beef, and chicken with a variety of vegetables. Although there is no firm recipe for this concoction, it is said it should be thick enough that a spoon will stand straight up in the bowl. Colonel Edward Bradley of Idle Hour Farm named Burgoo King, winner of the 1932 Kentucky Derby, in honor of a friend who made this great stew.

39 Hosting Your Own
Derby Party

It can be as informal as inviting your friends over to watch the Kentucky Derby on TV, or you can go all out and re-create the event in your own home. Hold a hat contest and encourage guests to wear costumes. Perhaps you can find some jockey silks on eBay or a red bugler's jacket with black riding boots. It's easy to make programs with the vital information for each horse, and your betting window can be as simple as your guests' names and the horses' post positions dropped in a basket with $2 wagers—winner takes all. There have to be roses, mint juleps, and pie, and for a main course fried chicken or burgoo. You can order Kentucky Derby napkins and plates, and even a recording of the sounds of the Derby. Whatever you choose, it's a great excuse to gather your friends and celebrate spring and horses on the first Saturday of May.

Burgoo King in the winner's circle with his jockey, Eugene James, May 7, 1932

40 Derby-Pie®

As sugar cubes and peppermints are to horses, Derby-Pie® is to the true Derby fan.

The traditional dessert of the Kentucky Derby was first served over a half century ago at the Melrose Inn in Prospect, Kentucky. George Kern, the manager of the restaurant, developed the recipe with the help of his parents, Walter and Leaudra.

What to name the pie was a much-discussed topic among the Kern family, and when they couldn't agree, the name Derby-Pie® was pulled out of a hat.

The name—and the pie—proved to be a winner. Each year during the month leading up to the Derby, Kern's Kitchen, Inc., sells more than 50,000 pies. Dark chocolate, walnuts, and a light flaky crust are the main ingredients, but the actual recipe for the trademarked pie remains a closely guarded secret of the Kern family.

It's always a staple at Derby parties. If you want the real thing, check out derbypie.com for a selection of retailers who will deliver this sumptuous pie right to your door.

"In action he was a glorious sight;
few thoroughbreds have exhibited such a
magnificent, sweeping, space-annihilating
stride, or carried it with such strength and
precision. His place is among the
Titans of the American turf."

—Salvator, *Daily Racing Form*

41
Omaha

The son of Triple Crown winner Gallant Fox, Omaha was born at Claiborne Farm in 1932 and owned by William Woodward of Belair Stud in Maryland. He was trained by Sunny Fitzsimmons, who also trained his sire. As a two-year-old, Omaha won only one race, but as a more mature three-year-old, he won the Derby and the Triple Crown under Canadian jockey Smokey Saunders.

With much hoopla the next year, he was sent to England in an attempt to raise his value as a super horse. He won the Queen's Plate, but then, with great media attention, he was beaten by a nose in the Ascot Gold Cup by a filly named Quashed.

Omaha returned home and was retired to stud at Claiborne Farm, then eventually moved to upstate New York. He did not appear to be a great stallion, and it wasn't until his fourth generation that the greatness of his bloodlines again became apparent in his siring of the great British champion Nijinsky II.

In 1950, he was retired to a farm outside the actual city of Omaha and was often taken to Omaha's racetrack, Ak-Sar-Ben, and led before the stands to be cheered by fans. Children were allowed to give him carrots and apples and have their photos taken sitting on his back.

When Omaha died in 1959 at age 27, he was buried at the racetrack and a monument was placed over his grave. When Ak-Sar-Ben closed in 1995, the memorial was put in storage, but during construction on the site, his remains were lost. In the summer of 2009, his monument was resurrected in a green space in Stinson Park, within an area of Omaha now called Aksarben Village.

42 War Admiral

Samuel Riddle was not a fan of the Kentucky Derby. He thought it was too long a race too early in the year for a three-year-old horse, and he had issues with Kentucky racing. Due to this, he did not run his legendary Man o'War in the 1920 Derby and instead sent him off to win the Preakness and Belmont Stakes. When Man o'War was 16, Riddle decided to breed him to his young mare Brushup based on the findings of a noted geneticist, Luther Burbank, who stated that the greatest offspring are produced by old men and young women. The foal this matchup produced was War Admiral.

Unlike his sire, War Admiral was a small horse. Taking after his dam, he stood at only 15.2 hands. A well-muscled dynamo, he was entirely brown, carrying neither the brilliant red coat nor the white markings of his sire, but inheriting both his personality and his heart. Both Man o'War and War Admiral had a disdain for people, bridles, and saddles. When his jockey Charley Kurtsinger was boosted up, War Admiral was in charge, and this willful horse delayed the start of the 1937 Kentucky Derby for a full eight minutes, refusing to line up for the starter's bell. He then went on to win by nearly two lengths.

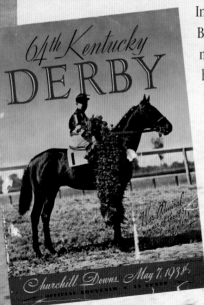

In the Preakness, War Admiral won by a head, and in the Belmont Stakes, after again holding up the start for eight minutes and tripping at the beginning of the race, he broke his sire's track record by a full length. When he was led into the winner's circle, it was found that he had broken this record while running on a broken hoof.

The Kentucky Derby, the Preakness, the Belmont, the Jockey Gold Cup—his list of victories goes on and on, yet War Admiral's most famous race was the one he lost—the much-heralded match race with West Coast star Seabiscuit, a grandson of Man o'War.

War Admiral is shown during a workout with jockey Charley Kurtsinger at Pimlico in Baltimore, Maryland, on October 26, 1938.

43 "The Master"

Eddie Arcaro is the only jockey to win the Triple Crown twice—on Whirlaway in 1941 and Citation in 1948—and was the jockey for the mount named Horse of the Year 11 times. Riding in 21 Kentucky Derbies, Arcaro won five times, came in second three times and third twice, and won the Belmont and the Preakness six times each. He had record earnings of more than $30 million when he retired in 1962.

In Citation's Kentucky Derby, Arcaro gave part of his purse to the widow of Al Snider, Citation's original jockey, who had drowned earlier that year. Years earlier, Arcaro had helped found the Jockeys' Guild, which provides aid and insurance to self-employed riders.

44 Calumet Farm

In its first 50 years, Calumet Farm became the Camelot of horse racing. Named for founder William Monroe Wright's famous Calumet Baking Powder, the farm's crimson-and-white barns still stand on the green rolling hills abutting Keeneland racetrack. As you pass through the crimson wrought-iron gates up the tree-lined lane, it is as if you are being invited into a fairy tale of famous horses—and you are. Calumet bred nine Kentucky Derby winners, two of them Triple Crown winners, and has had 11 horses elected to the National Thoroughbred Racing Hall of Fame. Much of this success has been attributed to Warren Wright, Sr.'s incredible horse sense in purchasing the sire Bull Lea, and in hiring Ben A. and Jimmy Jones as trainers and Eddie Arcaro as Calumet's primary jockey.

As in many fairy tales, Calumet Farm later fell into bankruptcy and scandal at the hands of a less scrupulous relative, but it was later saved by Henryk de Kwiatkowski. For a great read, this intriguing story is chronicled in the page-turner *Wild Ride: The Rise and Fall of Calumet Farm Inc., America's Premier Racing Dynasty* by Ann Hagedorn Auerbach.

45 Plain Ben

Every Derby program lists several great horse trainers, but no trainer has outperformed Ben A. Jones. Raised on a cattle farm in Missouri, Jones was a rascal who rode in the bush circuit and was always looking for a bet. Traveling around the country from fair to fair and also riding at the notorious track in Juarez, Mexico, he eventually landed in Kansas, where he trained the horse Lawrin, winner of the 1938 Kentucky Derby.

The following year, he was hired by Warren Wright of Calumet Farm. The first Calumet horse Jones ran in the Derby was Whirlaway, who won the Triple Crown in 1941. He sent out Derby winner Pensive in 1944, Triple Crown winner Citation in 1948, and Ponder and Hill Gail to win the Derby in 1949 and 1952, respectively. Jones then handed over the reins to his son Jimmy Jones, who won the 1957 Derby with Iron Liege and the 1958 Derby with Tim Tam.

46 Whirlaway

Whirlaway had a habit of zigzagging down the track, running wide and infuriating everyone who worked with him. It required three strong men to put a saddle on his back, a bolder man to sit in the saddle, and a man with the patience of a saint to train him. That man was Ben A. Jones. As the story goes, after weeks of leading Whirlaway along the rail, Jones devised a one-eyed blinker for the horse and then asked jockey Eddie Arcaro to gallop him through a slim opening along the rail created by Jones on his track pony. It appears that both Jones and Whirlaway overcame their fears, as Jones survived and Whirlaway won the 1941 Derby and the Triple Crown.

Whirlaway with jockey Eddie Arcaro and trainer
Ben A. Jones at Churchill Downs on May 3, 1941

47 A Stable of Celebrities

Most celebrities attend the Kentucky Derby dressed to the hilt with an equally glamorous companion on their arm, but some come with their own racing silks and a horse in hand.

In 1943, Eddie Anderson, who played Rochester on *The Jack Benny Show*, entered Burnt Cork. When his horse came in last, he announced he would ride his horse back to California. Hearing of this, Jack Benny, in his deadpan style, said, "He'd make better time if his horse rode him." No one knows if Benny had wagered any of his tightly held cash.

Elizabeth Arden, racing under the name Elizabeth Graham, won the 1947 Kentucky Derby with her horse Jet Pilot.

In 1992, several celebrities threw their hat in the ring. MC Hammer entered the befittingly named Dance Floor. Film producer Albert Broccoli brought along Brocco, and Berry Gordy of Motown Records had Powis Castle in the race. Burt Bacharach ran Soul of the Matter and, in 1995, returned with Afternoon Deelites.

George Steinbrenner, owner of the New York Yankees, brought six horses to the Derby between 1977 and 2005. Rick Pitino, basketball coach at the University of Louisville, entered Hallory Hunter in 1998 and A. P. Valentine in 2001 as part owner.

A consortium of owners that included film directors Gary Ross, Steven Spielberg, and Frank Marshall ran Atswhatimtalknbout in 2003, just after the completion of Ross's filming of *Seabiscuit*.

Director Steven Spielberg studying his racing program on Derby Day, 2003

Fourth Street Live

One of the hip and happening places in Louisville for the young at heart on Derby weekend is Fourth Street Live, a section of downtown Fourth Street jammed with restaurants, music halls, and bars. A stage in the middle of the street hosts free concerts into the wee hours. There's no easier spot to join in the Derby dance!

"To win the Triple Crown you've got to have a special horse.
You need speed and stamina and character, and the will to win.
Count Fleet had the character, or personality.
Whatever it was, he had it, breeding and the mind to win.
He loved the people around him, especially Mrs. Hertz.
Count Fleet was her pet, her baby."

—Johnny Longden, jockey

49 Count Fleet

The 1943 Triple Crown winner, Count Fleet, almost didn't race under the Hertz colors. Reigh Count, his 1928 Derby–winning sire, had not produced many winners, and John Hertz didn't like the looks of this unruly colt. He was up for sale, but there were no takers. As a two-year-old he behaved badly, bumping other horses only to lose the race, but by the end of this two-year-old campaign Count Fleet had won 10 of 15 races and had never been out of the money.

As a three-year-old, Count Fleet won every race. He was so formidable that jockey Johnny Longden routinely began to pull him in at the 16th pole rather than spend the horse's energy. In the Kentucky Derby, he loped along in front of the pack to win by three lengths. In the Preakness, Longden again slowed the horse as they won by eight lengths. In the Belmont Stakes, the top horses dropped out, and with only two opponents, trainer Don Cameron, Hertz and his wife, and Longden decided to just let Count Fleet loose and show his fans how fast he could run. No one thought he would break any records without competition, but he broke War Admiral's record for the Belmont Stakes and crossed the wire 25 lengths in front of the other horses. The son of a Derby winner, Count Fleet went on to sire one himself—Count Turf.

50 Johnny Longden

In his 40-year career, Johnny Longden took his horses to the winner's circle an amazing 6,032 times, making him the winningest jockey in history—until Bill Shoemaker surpassed the record in 1970.

Best known for his rides on the legendary Count Fleet, Longden was a legend himself, becoming the only person to win the Kentucky Derby as both a jockey and a trainer. Within three years of retiring as a rider, Longden stood in the Kentucky Derby winner's circle as trainer of the 1969 winner, Majestic Prince. As if that weren't enough, Longden helped organize, with Eddie Arcaro and Sam Resnick, the Jockeys' Guild to protect fellow riders.

At left, Count Fleet with Johnny Longden up, May 22, 1943

51
The Cosmetic Kid

Cosmetics mogul Elizabeth Arden had a stable of thoroughbreds and a stable of trainers. Although no trainer ever denied that Arden loved her horses or that they weren't well compensated, they came and went partially by whim and partially due to her unusual requests. Her horses were draped in pink cashmere horse blankets, and the grooms were asked to rub her eight-hour cream into their coats to make them shine. Fresh flowers were hung in the aisles of the barn, and she insisted that her perfumes be sprayed in the stalls. Her jockeys were not allowed to use whips, and if a horse wasn't pretty enough, it was dismissed even if it was fast.

In 1947, she won the Kentucky Derby with her horse Jet Pilot, nicknamed "the Cosmetic Kid," and her new trainer, Tom Smith of Seabiscuit fame. "Silent Tom" was a perfect fit for Arden as he said little, listened to her requests, bent to those that seemed somewhat reasonable, and silently did as he pleased when they weren't. His quiet, gentle ways of working with horses mesmerized her.

We don't know if Jet Pilot appeared in the winner's circle with lipstick on his muzzle, but it was Arden's habit to kiss her horses on the nose before the post parade.

Jet Pilot, with jockey Eric Guerin up, stands in the winner's circle, May 3, 1947.

Blue Grass

BREATH OF SPRING

There is a young, keen freshness about the fragrance of Blue Grass . . . the very spirit of Spring itself, with all its hope and promise . . . captured, as by magic in this world-famous perfume. Naturally it is

THE PERFECT EASTER GIFT

BLUE GRASS PERFUME, 3.75, 6.50, 12.00, 20.00, 32.50, 60.00
BLUE GRASS FLOWER MIST, 1.50, 2.50, 4.50
BLUE GRASS EAU DE TOILETTE, 5.00, 10.00
BLUE GRASS DUSTING POWDER, 1.50 (*prices plus taxes*)

Elizabeth Arden

"Treat a horse like a woman and
a woman like a horse and
they'll both win for you."

—Elizabeth Arden

52 Millionaires Row

When riding the escalator up to Millionaires Row, prepare to see more than just a great horse race. It is the choice seating for the likes of Michael Jordan, Donald Trump, and Jack Nicholson. Waiters will serve a lavish meal, and when it's time for the races, you can stroll out onto the balcony for a bird's-eye view of the racing oval.

In 2003, Churchill Downs added the Jockey Club Suites. These private rooms with all the amenities can be rented for corporate or family events. For other high rollers, there is the Gold Room on the sixth floor of Churchill Downs. The Turf Club is a "members only" venue, but there's still time to make a new friend before the next Derby.

53 Presidential Races

Several U.S. presidents have attended the Kentucky Derby, but only one while he was in office. During his campaign in 1968, Richard Nixon attended and cheered in Dancer's Image, ironically the only Derby winner who was later disqualified. Forward Pass, who ran second, was later declared the winner. Nixon announced at the race that he would return to the Derby in 1969 if he won the election. In 1969, he returned victorious with Gerald Ford and Ronald Reagan to watch Majestic Prince cross the wire.

Harry S. Truman once attended the Derby, and in 1952 Lyndon Johnson came. In 2000, George W. Bush arrived with his father, George H. W. Bush. Gerald Ford loved the Derby, and he and his wife, Betty, attended several times during his retirement. In 1983, both Jimmy Carter and George H. W. Bush came; the winner was Sunny's Halo.

"Assault was all heart.
He was just better than
all the horses around."

—Warren Mehrtens, jockey

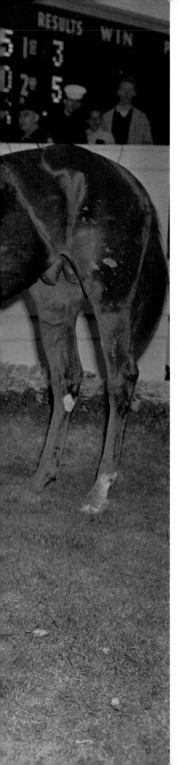

54 Assault

In 1942 at the King Ranch in Texas, the delicate broodmare Igual was bred to its thoroughbred stallion, Bold Venture, producing the legendary colt Assault. Assault was also a delicate horse, plagued by illness his entire life. As a foal, he stepped on a sharp object that split his right front hoof and had to have it cut away, necessitating a special shoe. To compensate for his malformed hoof, Assault developed an awkward gait at the walk and trot. No one thought he would amount to much. When Max Hirsch began Assault's training as a two-year-old, he was astonished to find that the horse had no awkwardness at a gallop.

In 1945, Assault made a lackluster debut as a two-year-old, winning only two of nine starts. As a three-year-old, he began to mature, and in front of an astounded crowd who had watched him "limp" through the post parade, Assault won the Wood Memorial. He then dismally lost the Derby Trial and was only an outside chance for the Kentucky Derby.

Nicknamed "the Club-footed Comet" by race fans, poor Assault not only had to overcome his physical ailments and erratic performance but also the prejudice of horsemen as he came from Texas. No horse from Texas, especially one raised at a cattle and quarter-horse ranch, could beat the famous Kentucky-bred horses. Assault and jockey Warren Mehrtens settled that argument by sailing under the wire of the 1946 Kentucky Derby eight lengths in the lead. Assault proved to have a heart as large as the Lone Star State and went on to win the Preakness and the Belmont Stakes, becoming the seventh winner of the Triple Crown.

Wearing a garland of roses, Assault stands in the Kentucky Derby winner's circle on May 4, 1946, with Mrs. Robert J. Kleberg Jr., jockey Warren Mehrtens, and owner Robert J. Kleberg Jr. of King Ranch, Texas.

55 Citation

Citation couldn't have had a better team to seal his name in history as a "wonder horse." Breeder and owner Warren Wright of Calumet Farm bred two Triple Crown winners, and he and his training team, Ben A. and Jimmy Jones, took five horses to the Kentucky Derby winner's circle. Yet this team and jockey Eddie Arcaro thought Citation was the greatest racehorse they'd ever seen. After all, he was a Calumet Farm foal sired by the legendary Bull Lea.

Citation won the Triple Crown as a three-year-old after being named champion two-year-old in 1947. At age two, his only defeat was to Bewitch, his stablemate at Calumet Farm. At age three, he won 17 stakes races in one year. At age four, he developed arthritis in his fetlock but was not put to stud, just brought home, rested, and treated for a year at Calumet Farm. Ben Jones and Wright had one more goal for this horse—to become the first horse to win $1 million. Wright didn't live to see this feat, but his wife, Lucille Parker Wright, asked Ben Jones to race him again to fulfill her husband's dream. At age five, Citation returned to the track, and at six he became the first horse to earn more than $1 million in his career.

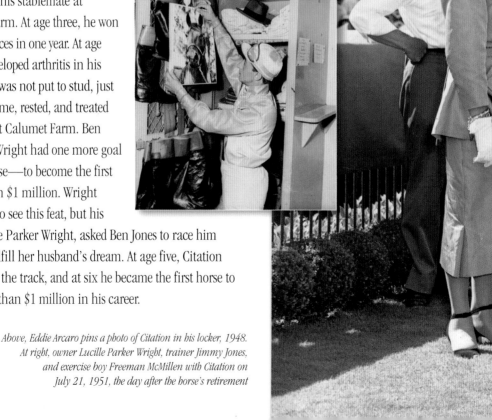

Above, Eddie Arcaro pins a photo of Citation in his locker, 1948.
At right, owner Lucille Parker Wright, trainer Jimmy Jones,
and exercise boy Freeman McMillen with Citation on
July 21, 1951, the day after the horse's retirement

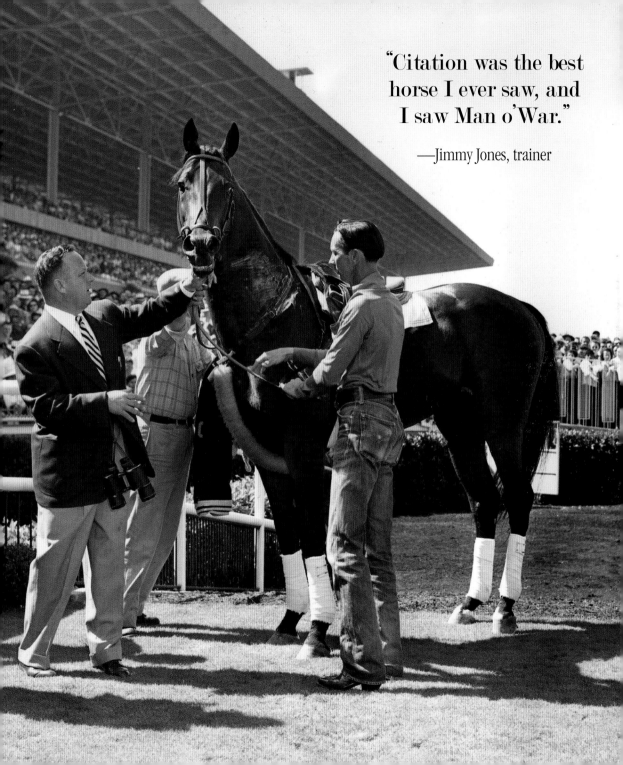

"Citation was the best horse I ever saw, and I saw Man o' War."

—Jimmy Jones, trainer

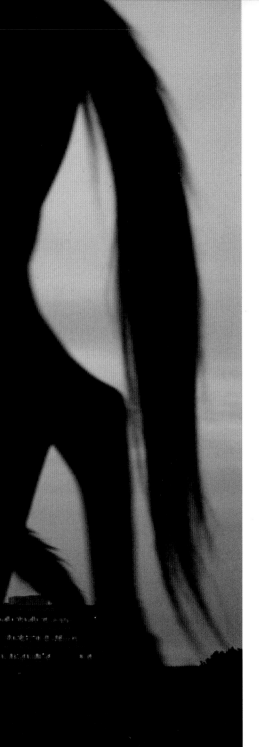

56
Dawn at the Downs

Monday through Thursday of Derby week, Churchill Downs opens its gates from 7 AM to 9 AM for visitors. You can stand at the rail in the comradeship of other Derby fans and watch morning workouts. You are actually close enough to see the horses' breath in the morning air and hear the rhythms of their exertion.

As if this isn't enough, breakfast is available at the lower clubhouse, and announcers are provided to keep you abreast of who is on the track and the times of the workouts. For those who have tickets and can rise early enough to dress up, Millionaires Row is also open and provides a gourmet breakfast buffet and a bird's-eye view of the track.

Arriving at the Derby Ball

A tradition that began in the 1920s at the Seelbach Hotel, the official Derby Ball is now held at the Galt House two weeks before the Kentucky Derby. During an evening of fine dining and dancing, the Queen of the Derby Festival is crowned, chosen by the spin of a wheel from the six selected princesses. The Queen and her court act as goodwill ambassadors for the 70 events leading up to the Derby, and each receives a college scholarship.

58
Parties, Parties, Parties!

During the two weeks leading up to the Kentucky Derby, there is a party everywhere you turn. If you wish to make a charitable donation to a cancer society, children's educational program, or an organization to help injured jockeys or retired thoroughbreds, and also want to have a great time and hobnob with celebrities, there is a black-tie affair for you. Held at the Seelbach, the Galt House, the Brown, the Kentucky Derby Museum, the Churchill Downs infield, Millionaires Row, private horse farms in the countryside, and everywhere else, benefits during Derby Week raise thousands of dollars for good causes.

If you don't own a tux, there are also parties at local bars and pubs, friends' homes, campgrounds, and the riverbank. On the morning of Derby Day, the governor of Kentucky throws an enormous ham-and-biscuit breakfast picnic for the public on the grounds of the capitol in Frankfort.

59
The Great Balloon Race

If you lift your head from your *Daily Racing Form* the weekend before the Kentucky Derby, you will be greeted by masses of colorful hot-air balloons floating through the sky. Louisville hosts the Great Balloon Race as a Kentucky Derby Festival event, using the "hare and hound" format. The "hare" balloon drifts out and drops a large fabric "X" in the countryside, and the other balloons try to pass over it and drop bags of Kentucky bluegrass seed on the "X." Sorry. There's no pari-mutuel betting.

The Derby Queen and her court, 1976

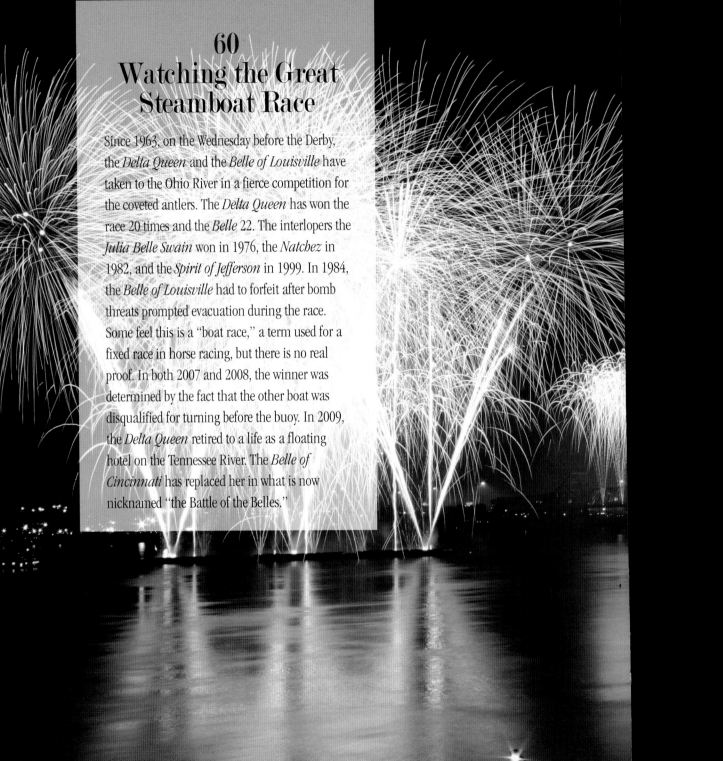

60
Watching the Great Steamboat Race

Since 1963, on the Wednesday before the Derby, the *Delta Queen* and the *Belle of Louisville* have taken to the Ohio River in a fierce competition for the coveted antlers. The *Delta Queen* has won the race 20 times and the *Belle* 22. The interlopers the *Julia Belle Swain* won in 1976, the *Natchez* in 1982, and the *Spirit of Jefferson* in 1999. In 1984, the *Belle of Louisville* had to forfeit after bomb threats prompted evacuation during the race. Some feel this is a "boat race," a term used for a fixed race in horse racing, but there is no real proof. In both 2007 and 2008, the winner was determined by the fact that the other boat was disqualified for turning before the buoy. In 2009, the *Delta Queen* retired to a life as a floating hotel on the Tennessee River. The *Belle of Cincinnati* has replaced her in what is now nicknamed "the Battle of the Belles."

The kickoff event of the two-week Kentucky Derby Festival is a pyrotechnic display—considered by many to be the best in the country. Barges jam-packed with fireworks hover under the Second Street Bridge. At 9:30 PM the Thunder begins to roll, ending in a mile-long cascading firefall into the river below.

62
Racing in Bed?

If you lack the athleticism ever to sit
astride a galloping thoroughbred,
perhaps you could enter the Kentucky
Derby Festival Bed Race on the Monday
evening prior to Derby Day at the
Kentucky Exposition Center. All that is
required is a $50 entry fee, a love of
theater and costume, a bed on wheels with a steering mechanism, a
driver, and four team members to push. If you're the winner, you get to
be bed-ridden in the Pegasus Parade!

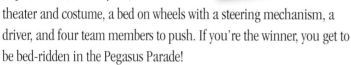

63
Standing in the Shadow
of Absolutely Pegasus

The Pegasus Parade began in 1956 as part of the Kentucky Derby Festival.
If you snag a good location, you can watch as the giant Pegasus balloon
looms overhead; local business owners wave from their floats, and
marching bands snap their spats and swing their tubas while tens of
horse brigades proudly prance, swing their tails, and splat the pavement.
This energetic, beautiful parade is held in downtown Louisville on the
Thursday evening before Derby Day.

Canonero II, far left, with jockey Gustavo Avila up, flies down the track to victory in the 97th Kentucky Derby, May 1, 1971.

64
The Venezuelan Mystery Horse

When a $1,200 Venezuelan colt arrived at the grounds of Churchill Downs with a trainer and handlers who spoke only Spanish, the guards didn't want to let them in. No one had ever heard of Canonero II, and the underweight colt with a crooked leg didn't look like a Derby contender. Canonero II had shipped from Venezuela after boarding three different planes: one that returned with an engine on fire, one that went back due to mechanical problems, and finally one full of cackling chickens being flown to Miami. When he landed, his papers weren't in order, and the horse had to endure a week of quarantine in a small stall with no exercise. After the 24-hour van ride from Miami, the horse had lost 70 pounds and was a nervous wreck. His trainer, Juan Arias, bedded him down and, to the ridicule of other contenders, whispered and talked to him, walked him, and loped him around the track bareback. Arias was quoted as saying, "I find that you must treat horses like women, speaking softly to them, and knowing when to give them love pats."

The 1971 Derby field was so large that the six horses of lowest merit were grouped together as one wager. Canonero II, of course, was put in this group. With his Venezuelan jockey, Gustavo Avila, aboard, Canonero II broke slowly, ran wide, and sailed past the favorites to win the Kentucky Derby.

In Venezuela, there was a national celebration, and his trainer declared him "the champion of all the people—black and white, rich and poor, American and Venezuelan, everyone." Canonero II went on to win the Preakness in the record time of 1:54 and became a favorite everyman's horse.

65
Studying the
Daily Racing Form at Wagner's

To soak in the feeling of what it's like to be a regular at Churchill Downs, stroll across the street to Wagner's Pharmacy and treat yourself to a fried egg or Derby sandwich. Eavesdrop on the backside gossip or ask a famous trainer to pass the salt. You may even get an inside tip on the Derby. There's nothing fancy about Wagner's but its walls are covered with Derby winner's circle photos—and, oh, if those walls could talk. Wagner's also manages the trackside kitchen on the backside.

Each year, Wagner's produces its own Derby cup, listing on the back the horses that finished last.

66
Reading All About It

Through the *Daily Racing Form*, the *Blood-Horse,* and the *Thoroughbred Times*, you can follow your favorites from their maiden races to their successes in the breeding shed. Each publication reports on the world of horse racing from a different angle, and whether you glean a hot tip for the Derby or a broader understanding of the economics of the industry, they'll all help you learn to talk the talk of an aspiring railbird.

Bill Shoemaker, one of the world's greatest jockeys, brought a winner across the line four times in the Kentucky Derby: Swaps in 1955, Tomy Lee in 1959, Lucky Debonair in 1965, and Ferdinand in 1986. At age 54, his victory on Ferdinand made him the oldest jockey ever to win the Kentucky Derby. Ironically, Bill Shoemaker's most-remembered Derby was aboard Gallant Man in 1957, when he misjudged the finish line and stood in his stirrups, losing the race to Bill Hartack on Iron Liege. He retired in 1990 with a record-setting 8,833 wins.

68 Bill Hartack

Bill Hartack won the Kentucky Derby on five different horses: Iron Liege in 1957, Venetian Way in 1960, Decidedly in 1962, Northern Dancer in 1964, and Majestic Prince in 1969. In 1958, he just missed being the only jockey to win the Kentucky Derby six times when he broke his leg and couldn't ride Tim Tam in the race.

Bill Hartack

"If Jack Nicklaus can win the Masters at 46,
I can win the Kentucky Derby at 54."

—Bill Shoemaker

69 The California Comet

In 1958, the biggest celebrity to attend the Derby was a horse named Silky Sullivan. Making his fame in California, Silky was a true closer, dropping so far back in his races that Bill Shoemaker complained he couldn't even see the field. But Silky was such a smart horse, he knew when to make his move. He once won a 6½-furlong race after being 40 lengths off the lead. He was a media star with features in *Sports Illustrated* and *Time*, and his "own" newspaper column and TV show.

After Silky won the Santa Anita Derby from 28 lengths back, his trainer, Reggie Cornell, was sure he could win the Kentucky Derby. CBS thought so, too. A special split-screen broadcast was devised so the camera could follow Silky as well as the rest of the field.

During the call, Silky was mentioned more times than the winner, Tim Tam. But the 1958 track was wet, and Silky didn't like mud. Dropping back 32 lengths off the lead, Silky only made it to 20 lengths off the lead and finished 12th. Perhaps his agents had told him it's not good to appear in the winner's circle with mud in your eye.

Silky Sullivan, far left, trails the pack in the 1958 Kentucky Derby.

70 Closers

A closer is a horse that prefers to run at the back of the field and make his move late in the race, picking off the competition one by one. Backing a true closer is a nerve-racking experience: Will he move in time; can he avoid traffic problems; will he have anything left in the stretch? In 1949, fans pondered all these questions as the Calumet colt Ponder was running dead last early in the race. After six furlongs he was 12th, but by the far turn he was sixth. In the stretch, he turned on the speed and was under the wire ahead of the field by an incredible three lengths. In 2009, 51–1 long shot Mine That Bird trailed in 19th place until the last half mile, when he began to thread the needle, weaving through traffic on the rail to win by 6¾ lengths. That's horse racing!

71 Secretariat

Sometimes the future is determined by a flip of a coin. The Phipps family offered to waive the stud fee of their stallion Bold Ruler in return for a choice of foals from successive breedings of two Meadow Stable mares, Hasty Matelda and Somethingroyal. A coin toss would decide who received first choice of foals. In the first year, a filly and a colt were produced, and in the next year's mating, Somethingroyal settled and Hasty Matelda came up barren. A decision was made that whoever won the toss would get first choice of foals, and the loser would receive the remaining foal and the yet-unborn foal of Somethingroyal. In 1969, Ogden Phipps called tails, won the toss, and chose the filly out of Somethingroyal. Penny Chenery was left with the colt out of Hasty Matelda and next year's Somethingroyal foal. On March 30, 1970, Somethingroyal gave birth to a brilliant red colt, eventually named Secretariat.

Secretariat was named Horse of the Year as a two-year-old and as a three-year-old went into the Kentucky Derby as the favorite. Faithfully cared for by groom Eddie Sweat, trained by Lucien Laurin, and ridden by Ron Turcotte, Secretariat not only won the 1973 Kentucky Derby, but won in the record time of 1:59.40 over his archrival Sham. In the Preakness, he won again, and it is often asserted he broke the record there, but the official timer malfunctioned. In the Belmont Stakes, Secretariat won in record time and led the field by an amazing 31 lengths! Fans continue to watch the video of this race for the thrill of seeing him cross the finish line followed by several seconds of only track until the stragglers come home.

Secretariat appeared on the cover of *Sports Illustrated* and *Time* and was included as No. 35 in ESPN's "Top 100 Greatest Athletes of the 20th Century." Heads to tails, Secretariat was truly a "super horse."

72 The Draw

A lot rides on the post position a horse draws for the Derby. The gate will hold 20 contenders, and on the Wednesday before the Derby, trainers and owners gather to seal their fate. It's now a media event. The owners and trainers first draw a number, then in that order select their post by hanging their colors beneath the chosen post position number. Choices are made according to several factors: their horse's talents, some superstition mixed with Derby lore, and the slim possibilities left. Choosing an outside post adds extra distance to the race but may prevent getting trapped in traffic. Since the year 1900, the luckiest post positions have been No. 1 with 12 winners; No. 5 with 12; No. 4, No. 10, and No. 8 with 10 each; and No. 2 with nine wins. Only two horses have won from gate No. 20: Big Brown in 2008 and Clyde Van Dusen in 1929.

73 Watching It All on TV

For those who can't sit in the grandstand at Churchill Downs, television offers a variety of race-related programming. The first Kentucky Derby telecast was in 1949. Then, due to new management who feared TV would hurt track attendance, coverage ceased in 1950 and 1951. TV coverage returned in 1952 and has grown ever since. With the introduction of TV stations dedicated to horse racing, you now can watch all the important Derby preps and listen to daily analysis by handicappers, jockeys, trainers, and sportscasters. Turner Classic Movies has even run back-to-back horse-racing movies surrounding the event. The Wednesday prior, you can tune in to watch the draw for post position. On Derby Day, the pageantry begins with early morning programs on the morning line, historical film footage of prior champions, and earlier races at Churchill Downs intertwined with interviews and "up close and personals" on the various horses and their connections, leading up to the climax of the call to the post of the Kentucky Derby. So be sure to walk the dog early and get a spot on the couch. This is a full day of horse play.

Bob Baffert gives a thumbs up at the post position draw for the Kentucky Derby on April 28, 2004.

74 Seattle Slew

Purchased for only $17,500, Seattle Slew was a bargain as a first and awkward foal by Bold Reasoning out of My Charmer. He was nicknamed "Baby Huey" due to the way he ran, throwing one foot to the side, but as soon as training began, Seattle Slew outgrew all that. He won all three of his two-year-old races and was named 1976 champion two-year-old. Slew arrived at the 1977 Kentucky Derby as the hands-down favorite and won. Still undefeated, Seattle Slew won the Preakness at Pimlico, grazing the unofficial record. Facing a muddy track at Belmont, he led wire-to-wire and won by four lengths. Seattle Slew was Eclipse Horse of the Year as a three-year-old and was the first undefeated Triple Crown winner. In 1978, Seattle Slew ran against the 1978 Triple Crown winner Affirmed in the Marlboro Cup and won the race by three lengths.

Seattle Slew went on to sire most notably Landaluce, A. P. Indy, and Swale. One of his daughters produced the legendary Cigar. After an illustrious career, in 2002 at age 28, Seattle Slew passed away on the 25th anniversary of his win in the Kentucky Derby.

Jockey Jean Cruguet, aboard Seattle Slew, rises in the saddle and looks back as he crosses the finish line to win the 103rd Kentucky Derby, on May 7, 1977.

Affirmed, with jockey Steve Cauthen, crosses the finish line to win the 104th running of the Kentucky Derby, on May 6, 1978. Alydar, with jockey Jorge Velasquez (behind Affirmed in this photo), finished second. Believe It, No. 9, finished third.

75 Affirmed vs. Alydar

In 1977, two thoroughbreds came on the scene who would forever be linked by their rivalry. One was Affirmed, the other Alydar. Both of Native Dancer lineage, each had a different racing style. Affirmed liked to run toward the front, while Alydar was a closer. Affirmed broke his maiden by running wire to wire at Belmont Park. In his second race, he won the Youthful Stakes, with Alydar coming in fifth. This is the last time Alydar would suffer that humiliation. In July at Belmont in the Great American Stakes, Alydar beat Affirmed by 3½ lengths. They came together again in the Hopeful, and Affirmed won over Alydar by ½ length. In the Futurity, Affirmed squeezed out Alydar by a nose. Alydar won the Champagne Stakes, beating Affirmed by 1¼ lengths, but Affirmed returned to beat Alydar by a neck in the Laurel Futurity. The racing world couldn't get enough of this chess game, and many fans felt Alydar needed only a bit more distance to suit his closing style. The Kentucky Derby could provide such a race.

In his three-year-old season, Affirmed's trainer decided to avoid the frenzy of the rivalry by keeping his horse in California. Affirmed won the San Felipe Stakes, the Santa Anita Derby, and the Hollywood Derby. Meanwhile, Alydar, residing in Florida, won the Flamingo Stakes and the Florida Derby.

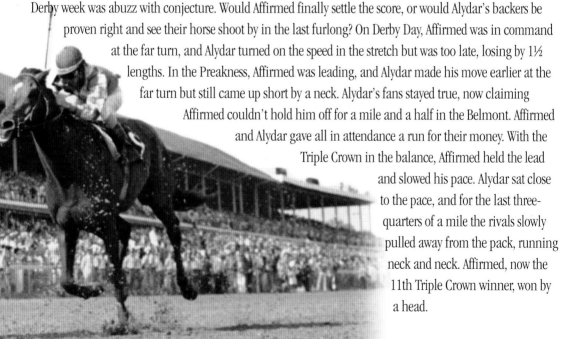

Derby week was abuzz with conjecture. Would Affirmed finally settle the score, or would Alydar's backers be proven right and see their horse shoot by in the last furlong? On Derby Day, Affirmed was in command at the far turn, and Alydar turned on the speed in the stretch but was too late, losing by 1½ lengths. In the Preakness, Affirmed was leading, and Alydar made his move earlier at the far turn but still came up short by a neck. Alydar's fans stayed true, now claiming Affirmed couldn't hold him off for a mile and a half in the Belmont. Affirmed and Alydar gave all in attendance a run for their money. With the Triple Crown in the balance, Affirmed held the lead and slowed his pace. Alydar sat close to the pace, and for the last three-quarters of a mile the rivals slowly pulled away from the pack, running neck and neck. Affirmed, now the 11th Triple Crown winner, won by a head.

"Only way that horses will win is if you sit there and spend time with 'em. Show 'em that you're tryin' to help 'em. Love 'em. Talk to 'em. Get to know 'em. You love 'em, and they'll love you, too."

—Eddie Sweat

76
Unsung Heroes

Behind all the adulation given to the winning thoroughbred on Derby Day is the person who rubbed and cajoled him as he learned to run, and fed and loved him long after the last rose had wilted. A thoroughbred's groom is his best friend, and without a great groom he will never see a garland of roses draped across his withers. Grooms work long hours with little monetary compensation and spare recognition. Most do it for the love of horses.

Willie Saunders, groom at Idle Hour Farm, tended to the needs of an astounding five Derby winners. He was the groom for Colonel E. R. Bradley, and he fed and cared for Behave Yourself, Bubbling Over, Burgoo King, and Broker's Tip. Saunders also was the groom to the legendary Swaps when he stood at Darby Dan Farm.

Eddie Sweat, groom to Riva Ridge and Secretariat, has recently been immortalized in the statue park at the Kentucky Horse Park, walking with a calm hand on "Big Red's" side, and in Lawrence Scanlan's book *The Horse That God Built*.

These are the people who know the real celebrities of the Kentucky Derby. They meet with them in the morning mist, and the evening dusk, and sometimes sleep by their stalls. They are the unsung heroes of the Kentucky Derby.

At left, Smarty Jones gets a morning bath from his groom.
At right, Secretariat is led by groom Eddie Sweat on May 5, 1973,
after winning the 99th Kentucky Derby.

77
When Winning Isn't Everything

One of the greatest horses ever to run in the Kentucky Derby was Native Dancer. In his two-year-old campaign he won all of his nine races and was named champion two-year-old and Horse of the Year. The year was 1952, and Native Dancer became a nation's hero through the medium of television. He was a beautiful gray, nicknamed "the Gray Ghost," who loved to stalk the pace. In 1953, he headed to the Kentucky Derby as the undefeated favorite—and lost. Fouled during the race, he rallied and came in second to Dark Star. Native Dancer won the Preakness, the Belmont, and the Travers Stakes and was named champion three-year-old. He won all three races he entered in 1954 and appeared on the cover of *Time* as Horse of the Year. In retirement, he was a successful sire, producing two Derby and one Kentucky Oaks winner. He won 21 of his 22 starts, his only loss being the Kentucky Derby.

At left, Dark Star beats Native Dancer by a head in the 1953 Derby.
Above, Native Dancer with Bernie Everson up at Belmont in 1954

97

The Ride of Your Life

The book title *Funny Cide: How a Horse, a Trainer, a Jockey, and a Bunch of High School Buddies Took on the Sheiks and Bluebloods...and Won* sums up the story. With limited funds, a group of friends, who had only dreamed of sitting in the owners' area and being on the backside of the track, started Sackatoga Stable—

named for their hometown of Sackets Harbor and Saratoga and with silks in their high school colors. When their first horse was lost in a claiming race to the tune of $62,500, they decided to invest this money in a horse with a bit more pedigree. Under the advisement of trainer Barclay Tagg, the friends purchased a gelding named Funny Cide at a bargain price. When he turned out to be very fast, they entered him in the Kentucky Derby. To the delight of the media, the group arrived at Churchill Downs in a rented Sackets Harbor school bus filled with excited friends and family. The biggest surprise was when Funny Cide and jockey Jose Santos ran between the two favorites, Empire Maker and Peace Rules, and won the 2003 Kentucky Derby.

A happier, more colorful crowd has never assembled in the winner's circle. Funny Cide was the first New York–bred horse to win. Sackatoga Stable arrived at Pimlico two weeks later in the yellow school bus to watch Funny Cide run the Preakness. He won that race, but on a muddy Saturday three weeks later he lost the Belmont Stakes.

Now retired, Funny Cide first became Barclay Tagg's beloved track pony and now resides in the Hall of Champions at the Kentucky Horse Park. This everyman's horse is now visited daily by fans from around the world.

Jockey Jose Santos aboard Funny Cide after crossing the finish line to win the 129th running of the Kentucky Derby on May 3, 2003.

79 Smarty Jones Mania

From mayhem to mania, Smarty Jones' hard-luck story captured a nation's imagination. After losing his first trainer to murder, Smarty Jones shattered his skull and eye socket in the starting gate while training. His owners, the Chapmans, had downscaled their already modest 100-acre farm to a smaller 11-acre spread, still wistfully retaining the name Someday Farm.

Winning his debut race at Philadelphia Park, Smarty Jones, piloted by Philadelphia Park jockey Stewart Elliot, went on to win all his races, including the Rebel and the Arkansas Derby. Oaklawn Park, celebrating its centennial, had offered a $5 million bonus to a horse that won these two races and the Kentucky Derby.

With a sassy name, a great story, and an undefeated record, the media and its audience couldn't get enough. Smarty's blue-and-white colors appeared on buttons, hats and T-shirts,

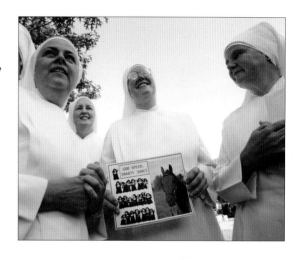

banners, and posters. A horse who loved the camera, Smarty would perk his ears and pose for the media attention. When he won the Kentucky Derby by 2¾ lengths, he became the first undefeated winner since Seattle Slew and, with the Oaklawn bonus, won an incredible $5.88 million! A record crowd amassed at Pimlico to watch Smarty win the Preakness by the largest margin in the race's history: 11½ lengths. By the last leg of the Triple Crown, the nation had developed full-blown Smarty mania. Belmont Park boasted record attendance at the Belmont Stakes as Smarty's fans watched their hero take the lead in the final stretch—only to be passed by Birdstone in the blink of an eye. The defeat was so stealthy that Smarty's fans retain disbelief to this day. He was retired to stud at Three Chimneys, and fans still flock to the farm to get a glimpse of their almost, "say it isn't so, Jones," Triple Crown hero.

Partying in the Infield

Rivaling Mardi Gras in New Orleans, the party in the infield at the Derby has become the cheap ticket to the event, although you may never see a horse once you get there. Once the desired vantage point for trainers to watch the race, the infield at the Derby teems with intoxicated revelers, and all eyes are out for nudity and antics. In 1918, the infield was planted with potatoes to help with the potato shortage, and in 1942, soldiers from Fort Knox were housed there. From military to mayhem, the infield carries a mystique of its own.

81
Doubling Your Pleasure

Held at the Barnstable mansion on Spring Street, the Doublemint Twins' Derby Eve Barnstable Brown Gala is considered the most star-studded party of them all. Priscilla and Patricia Barnstable, raising money for the Barnstable Brown Foundation for diabetes research, know how to bring out the rich and famous. Stargazers stake out spots hours early to watch guests arrive.

Mingling with the Rich and Famous

How many events can you attend where, over the years, you might have run into Michael Jordan, Wesley Snipes, Raquel Welch, Peyton Manning, Cybill Shepherd, Serena Williams, Smokey Robinson, ZZ Top, Chubby Checker, Charlie Rose, Anna Nicole Smith, Lynn Redgrave, Dennis Hopper, Robert Altman, Dan Aykroyd, George Strait, Bo Derek, Pamela Anderson, Bob Costas, Alice Cooper, Donald Trump, Teri Hatcher, Robert Duvall, Lee Iacocca, Morgan Freeman, Bob Hope, Jerry Lewis, Telly Savalas, Robert Goulet, Joe Namath, J. Edgar Hoover, Claudette Colbert, John Wayne, Zsa Zsa Gabor, Mikhail Baryshnikov, Joan Rivers, Muhammad Ali, Tony Bennett, Kid Rock, Ed Asner, Lana Turner, Don Ameche, Sigourney Weaver, Wynton Marsalis, Anjelica Huston, Rush Limbaugh, Jack Nicholson, Sylvester Stallone, Al and Tipper Gore, Waylon Jennings, Babe Ruth, Courteney Cox Arquette, Paris Hilton, or Francis Ford Coppola . . . to name but a few.

83
Royalty

An avid racing fan and owner of a racing stable, Queen Elizabeth II fulfilled her lifelong dream of attending the Kentucky Derby in 2007.

In 1974, Princess Margaret and her husband, Lord Snowdon, presented the trophy at the 100th running of the Derby. The Duke of Windsor was there in 1951, and in 1930 Edward George Villiers Stanley, the 17th Earl of Derby, attended. Lord Stanley was disappointed that he came during prohibition and wasn't able to sip a mint julep at the race.

At left, Paris Hilton attends the Barnstable Brown Derby party, May 1, 2009.
Above, Queen Elizabeth II chats with Prince Philip as actress Susan Lucci looks on
at the 133rd Kentucky Derby, May 5, 2007.

84 Artist Peter Williams

With his trademark cap and traveling easel, New Zealand native Peter Williams can be seen capturing Derby Day on canvas from the prestigious vantage point of the paddock.

85 Gazing at the Twin Spires

Perhaps the most recognized symbol in horse racing, the twin spires rise above the grandstand of Churchill Downs, adding an air of dignity and tradition to the sport. The eyes of every fan are immediately drawn upward to the spires; it is as if you are entering the cathedral of horse racing. Architect Joseph Dominic Baldez designed the hexagonal spires in 1895 while drawing the plans for the new grandstand. Adding to the historic significance, there are plaques beneath the spires on the paddock side commemorating each Derby winner that has passed beneath them and those that ran prior to their construction.

86 The Paddock

On Derby Day, the paddock area, festooned with roses, is the place to be as the trainers lead in their contenders to be saddled for the race. Fans engulf the surrounding fence, and the gatekeeper struggles to allow only the connections within the hallowed center circle of grass.

After the grooms and horses circle the paddock once or twice, each horse is led into its numbered stall, where the trainer lifts the saddle and tightens the girth and the jockey is given any final instructions. One by one, the silk-clad jockeys are legged up on their mounts at the call to the post, the procession under the twin spires, through the tunnel, to the starting gate, and on to their destiny.

87 The Call to the Post

A red-coated bugler with shining black boots and a glistening horn steps forward and plays the call to the post. As the clear sharp sound splits the air, the jockeys and horses leave the paddock and parade toward the track. This is the moment everyone is waiting for, announced as if the Angel Gabriel were a race fan.

88 All the Beautiful Horses

The post parade before the Derby can take your breath away. You are seeing some of the most athletic, well-groomed, finely tuned, pampered horses in the world. With gleaming coats and bright eyes, they prance along as bettors scramble to place their last-minute wagers. Bettors beware: A bay or dark bay/brown has won the Kentucky Derby more than 60 times, a chestnut 43, but the gray/roan has made only eight trips to the winner's circle.

"In the paddock the horses were led around and around the walking ring as they waited for the jockeys to be weighed in. People pushed and shoved to get close to the fence that surrounded the paddock, fighting for a glimpse of the horses, hoping to be able to choose the one that would go down in racing history as a Derby winner."

— Mildred Mastin Pace, *Old Bones the Wonder Horse*

89 The Break

A momentary hush comes over the crowd in anticipation of the break. The bell rings, the tote board freezes the odds, the Derby contenders leap from the mechanical starting gate to a deafening roar, and the gate crew stands in the dust watching history unfold.

A type of stall machine starting gate was introduced at the 1930 Kentucky Derby, won by Gallant Fox. Prior to that a web barrier was used, and for the first few Derbies horses milled behind a line drawn in the dirt until the starter was satisfied and rang the bell.

90 And They're Off!

As the thoroughbreds break from the gate, a voice pours over the cheering crowd. Perched high above the track, the announcer calls the race and tells the story as the jockeys and horses juggle for position on the track. This is not an easy job, and timing and flair are everything. Only six people have held this job at Churchill Downs, the sixth beginning in 2009. Chic Anderson is the most notable, being on scene for Seattle Slew's Derby, as well as calling the Belmont Stakes for Secretariat's 31-length victory. The caller of the race is as nervous as the horses in the gate, with only one chance to get it right.

Secretariat (horse 1A), with Ron Turcotte up, in the 99th Kentucky Derby, on May 5, 1973

KENTUCKY DERBY
122
MAY 4, 1996
OFFICIAL PHOTO FINISH
GRINDSTONE

WIN
TRACKMASTER

Churchill Downs Kentucky Derby

91 The Turns

Leaning out of your box, you strain your neck to see between the hats and catch the horses coming around the turn. The turns play an important part in the race, with riders rushing to get closer to the rail before the clubhouse turn, and later with the stalkers and the closers making their move on the turn for home.

92 The Stretch

It's hard not to hold your breath as the leaders enter the homestretch and race for the wire, pursued by fast-moving closers. In 1933, there was an actual "fighting finish," with the jockeys of the dueling Head Play and Broker's Tip grabbing at each other over the last three-sixteenths of the stretch. With judges unable to determine who started the fracas, Broker's Tip remained the winner and Head Play second. Both jockeys were suspended.

93 Wire-to-Wire Wins

At the Kentucky Derby, there have been eight wire-to-wire wins since 1950: Dark Star, Swaps, Kauai King, Riva Ridge, Bold Forbes, Spend A Buck, Winning Colors, and War Emblem. It takes an incredibly strong horse and a talented jockey to lead from the gate and still conserve the strength to stay ahead in the stretch. As you watch the motion of such a horse, it's as if some void is opening that must be filled, as if that thundering power is effortless.

94 Photo Finish

It's been said that Grindstone won the Derby in 1996 by a whisker as he moved past the favorite Cavonnier, at the wire. The photo finish gave him the nod, and Jerry Bailey and Grindstone headed to the winner's circle, leaving Chris McCarron and Cavonnier to head to the barn. The photo finish was introduced in the 1930s, first with a single camera that was tripped at the finish. Later a "slit" camera with no shutter was invented, which gave a more accurate image of the horses' positions, and now high-speed digital cameras are used.

95
Experiencing the Most Exciting Two Minutes in Sports

After getting up early for morning works and staying up late for Derby balls, you find yourself standing in your box wearing the perfect hat, holding a mint julep and hopefully the winning ticket, as the two weeks of the Derby Festival culminates in two exhilarating minutes from starting gate to finish wire.

(That is, unless you were watching Secretariat, who set the Derby record of 1:59.40, or Monarchos, who came close in 2001 at 1:59.97.)

Below, jockey Jerry Bailey rides Sea Hero to the finish line to win the 119th running of the Kentucky Derby, May 1, 1993.
At left, Monarchos, with Jorge Chavez up, crosses the finish line to win the 127th running of the Kentucky Derby, May 5, 2001.

96
The Finish Line

As you cheer your horse coming down the stretch,
the jockeys and horses are focused on the finish line.
With one last burst of speed, one last explosion of
energy, the finish line looms ahead. As the winner
passes under the wire and the jockey rises up in
celebration, the finish line acts as a demarcation
of hopes shattered and dreams fulfilled.

97
Holding the
Winning Ticket

With your throat dry from cheering, tears in your
eyes, and a smile on your face, you look down at
the winning ticket in your hand, and no matter
how large the payoff or whether you won by whim
or careful calculation, the greatest thing is to
know you're still lucky.

*Ferdinand crosses the finish line to win the
Kentucky Derby, May 3, 1986.*

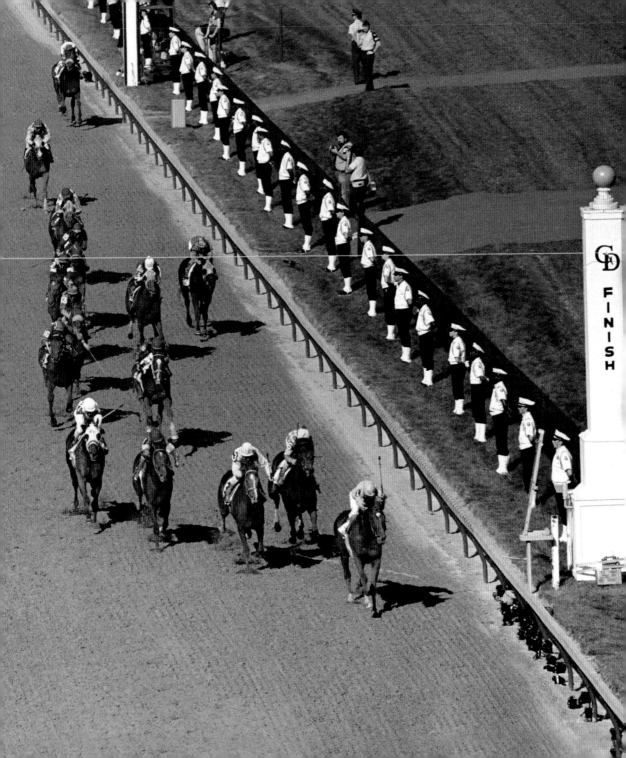

98 Going to the Winner's Circle

At dawn on Derby Day, the women from Kroger, who spent Derby Eve creating the rose garland, are standing in the winner's circle at Churchill Downs, filling the large urns with long-stemmed roses. As they watch the sunrise and hear the distant hoofbeats echo off the grandstand, the magic of the moment makes up for staying awake all night.

Many horses and owners step into a winner's circle at Churchill Downs during the racing season, but only for the Kentucky Derby does the winner pose in the revered Kentucky Derby winner's circle, located in the infield. Millions of dollars are gambled and hundreds of lives are dedicated to the dream of one day standing here by your horse or sitting here on your mount, with roses thrown over its withers, and knowing that you have won the greatest race in America.

The purse for the first Kentucky Derby, in 1875, was a guaranteed $1,000. It was raised to $1 million in 1996 and to $2 million in 2005. The winner receives 62 percent of the guaranteed purse plus all additional fees; the jockey gets 10 percent of the winner's share.

Below, Jerry Bailey atop Sea Hero in the winner's circle, May 1, 1993.
At left, Giacomo in the winner's circle, May 7, 2005.

99 Calvin Borel

Trailing far behind at the first turn, a small, brown 50–1 long shot piloted by a patient and courageous jockey stunned the crowd at the 2009 Kentucky Derby. Mine That Bird and Calvin Borel passed 18 horses in the last half mile by weaving the rail in 47.8 seconds, in perhaps the most daring ride of any Derby. One of the most emotional yet fearless riders in the game, Calvin Borel won the hearts of America with tears in his eyes as he praised his horse, the owner, the trainer, and his parents, who had recently passed away.

The day before, Borel had won the Kentucky Oaks by an astounding 20 lengths on Rachel Alexandra and going into the Preakness was already committed to ride her if she ran. Calvin rode Rachel Alexandra and beat Mine That Bird by one length. For the running of the Belmont, Borel was back on his Derby mount, Mine That Bird, with the possibility of being the first jockey to "win" the Triple Crown riding different horses.

Fans stood at the rail chanting Calvin's name as he and Mine That Bird tried their best, only to finish third to Summer Bird.

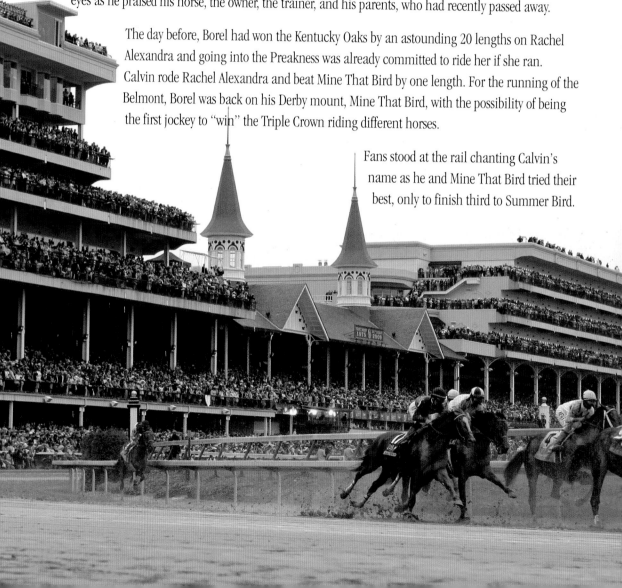

At left, Calvin Borel aboard Mine That Bird trails the entire field as the horses enter the first turn, May 2, 2009. At right, Borel pilots Mine That Bird to victory in the 135th Kentucky Derby.

"Someday he will be in the Hall of Fame, but he's already a legend among his peers."

—Gary Stevens, jockey

100
Remembering Barbaro

Winner of the 2006 Kentucky Derby, Barbaro sustained a life-threatening injury in the Preakness at Pimlico. Barbaro's owners and medical staff at the New Bolton Center did everything that could be done to save this horse. The tragedy spurred an outpouring of grief and hope from horse lovers around the world who followed Barbaro's progress through the Internet, television, and print. A Web site was set up where concerned fans could get hourly updates, see Barbaro in his stall, and learn of the heroic efforts to save him. Baskets of apples and carrots, good-luck charms, get-well wishes, and cards arrived daily at the clinic. Despite great strides in recovery, on January 29, 2007, Barbaro was euthanized after developing laminitis.

Barbaro's tragic death spurred the donation of millions of dollars to find a cure for laminitis. Large animal veterinarian scholarships were awarded, and a commission to study thoroughbred breeding practices that may be endangering the sturdiness of the breed has been established. Thank you, Barbaro.

In April 2009, a statue of Barbaro running to the finish line was unveiled over his grave in front of the Kentucky Derby Museum outside Gate 1 at Churchill Downs.

Barbaro, with Edgar Prado up, nears the finish line to win the Kentucky Derby, May 6, 2006.

Golden Works and her new filly
by Action This Day enjoy the
bluegrass at Rosecrest Farms in
Paris, Kentucky.

101
Hope

With a tick of the clock and the last refrains of "Auld Lang Syne," the anticipations of the new year begin again. By racing regulation, all thoroughbreds, no matter what date they were foaled, simultaneously turn a year older on New Year's Day. Foaling season is just around the corner, and it is time to look for possiblities at the yearling sales. The two-year-old racing campaigns will begin, and aspiring three-year-olds will be running in the Derby preps. While glasses are raised in a toast to both the past and the future, owners, trainers, breeders, and grooms wonder if the bright-eyed three-year-old in their stable will get the chance to break from the gate the first Saturday in May. Hope abounds as the champagne corks pop: a Kentucky Derby contender, a blanket of roses, perhaps the Triple Crown?

Acknowledgments

Many people opened doors and paddock gates to make the research for this book such a memorable experience. I want to thank my horse-racing cohort, Suzanne Gleeson, for her years of enthusiasm for traveling to races with me, her companionship in trips for this venture, and her incredible skills at fact-checking and knowing how to "talk the talk" for this book.

Thank you to my husband, Dick Klausner, for listening to endless Derby chatter and taking care of my horses while I was gone. I couldn't do much without him. Thank you to the staff at Prairie Lights Bookstore for giving me the time to work on this project.

I also wish to thank Kathleen Adams and Karyn and Colleen Pirrello for giving their time to provide access to many beautiful breeding farms. Thank you to Rosecrest Farm, Doug Arnold of Buck Pond Farm, Des Dempsey of Spendthrift Farm, and Jen Roytz at Three Chimneys for taking time out of their schedule to provide tours, talk, and access to photograph. A special thanks to Brian Van Steenbergh, exercise rider at Three Chimneys, for his insightful commentary on working with thoroughbred stallions.

Phyllis Rogers of the Keeneland Library deserves a trophy for her incredible enthusiasm. She has a way of making each visitor seem like an old friend. Thank you to curator Katherine Veitschegger for taking time during a very busy period at the Kentucky Derby Museum. I am indebted to Manny Cadima for all the work he puts into the Louisville Thoroughbred Club and his gracious offer to take me on the backstretch during Derby week. Thank you to all the people at the Kentucky Derby Festival for providing access to their wonderful events.

1941 KENTUCKY DERBY CHURCHILL DOWNS LOUISVILLE

Jack and Betty Adams and family once again outdid themselves in southern hospitality by providing shelter as well as sack lunches, rock-star Derby parking, and late night cocktails. Thank you.

Thanks go to train expert Stuart Slaymaker, for helping us unlock the secrets of the Derby train, to Ted Ciuzio of the Associated Press for providing so many great images, and to the High Society Resale Boutique in Scottsdale, Arizona, for providing our fabulous vintage outfits for both the Derby and the Oaks.

To our wonderful editor, Ann Stratton, who guided us through the turns with a steady hand on the reins, and to Leslie Stoker for continuing to believe that there are 101 reasons to love many things.

And finally, I want to thank my friend Mary Tiegreen, for providing the possibility to fulfill a childhood dream and deserving an Oscar for supporting cast. Not only is she a talented designer, but just a lot of fun. And we had fun!

Thank you to the women at Kroger, the guides at the Kentucky Derby Museum, the mint julep vendors, the staff at Wagner's, Wallace Station, the Brown, and the Seelbach, and, thank you, Chip Woolley, for giving me a rose from Mine That Bird's Derby garland!

A Tiegreen Book

Published in 2010 by Abrams Image
An imprint of ABRAMS

Library of Congress Cataloging-in-Publication Data:
Seggerman, Sheri.
  The Kentucky Derby : 101 reasons to love America's favorite horse race / Sheri Seggerman
& Mary Tiegreen.
     p. cm.
  ISBN 978-1-58479-809-5
  1. Kentucky Derby. 2. Kentucky Derby--Pictorial works. I. Tiegreen, Mary. II. Title.
  SF357.K4S44 2010
  798.4009769'44--dc22

                              2009029911

EDITOR: Ann Stratton
DESIGNER: Mary Tiegreen
PRODUCTION MANAGER: Tina Cameron

Abrams Image books are available at special discounts when purchased in quantity for premi-
ums and promotions as well as fundraising or educational use. Special editions can also be
created to specification. For details, contact specialsales@abramsbooks.com or the address
below.

Printed and bound in China
10 9 8 7

Photo credits:

AP IMAGES: pages 1, 2–3, 4, 14, 18, 19, 20, 28, 31, 34, 35, 36, 42, 43, 44, 47, 52–53, 54, 56,
58, 60, 61, 63, 65, 66, 68 (inset), 69, 70, 78, 82, 83, 86, 87, 89, 90–91, 92–93, 94, 95, 98,
99, 101, 102, 103, 104, 105, 106, 110–111, 112, 114 (inset), 115, 117, 118, 119, 120, 121,
122–123, 125, 128. THE KEENELAND LIBRARY: pages 16–17, 50, 84 (inset), 84–85, 96, 97.
THE NATIONAL MUSEUM OF RACING AND HALL OF FAME: page 33. THE KENTUCKY DERBY FESTIVAL:
pages 72, 77. KERN'S KITCHENS: pages 48 (insets), 48–49. ISTOCKPHOTO: pages 6–7, 23,
74–75. LIBRARY OF CONGRESS: pages 8–9, 37 (inset), 126–127. SHERI SEGGERMAN: pages 5, 15,
16 (inset), 22, 23 (insets), 26, 27, 38, 39, 41, 55, 59, 62 (inset), 71, 76 (inset), 80, 81, 100,
107, 124. MARY TIEGREEN: pages 9 (inset, from the collection of Mary Tiegreen), 10–11, 12–13,
13 (inset), 24 (inset), 25, 38, 40, 41, 52 (inset, from the collection of Mary Tiegreen), 109.

ABRAMS The Art of Books
195 Broadway, New York, NY 10007
abramsbooks.com